Truth, Will & Relevance

Shane.

Enjoy the book!

—Brian

Truth, Will & Relevance

Essays for a Generative Age
by **Brian Frank**

An **OPEN CONCEPTUAL** Book
yxu | MMX

Published by Open Conceptual in London, ON, Canada.
connect@openconceptual.com

ISBN: 978-0-9865591-0-5

Contents

1 Thinking Through History

Reading history makes me marvel at everyone's apparent stupidity. Even the "great" creators, leaders, and discoverers tended to miss the full importance of what they were doing. And then there are the not-so-great leaders and followers who tried standing in the future's way. It isn't so much that they're wrong, it's that they're completely oblivious to something essential. Of course, *we're* smarter... right?

There's a quote I keep revisiting in Arthur Schlesinger Jr.'s book about Franklin Roosevelt during the Great Depression. He observes that "we are always in a zone of imperfect visibility so far as the history just over our shoulder is concerned." [1]

Experts are still grappling over the causes and consequences of that economic crisis from the first half of the last century; how can we expect to fully understand our own? We have to proceed with whatever imperfect information and ideas we have. Developing ways to do that more effectively is what this book is about.

One of the reasons I look at history is we can actually make sense of it, whereas our own time will take decades to understand and explain. We need to know what happens next before we can fully appreciate the character and importance of what's happening now. The best we can do is get a sense of the longer-term undercurrents by looking a few decades further back, at what we *can* understand, and work from there.

When I tried making sense of the frenetic and uncertain world of work I was entering in 2000, I strained to find something stable. Everything was in flux. We'd gone from Dotcom hype to the Dotcom crash as people who thought the Internet would put them on the fast track to financial independence learned, well, it's a little more complex than that. Music, publishing, and advertising — unfortunately the three industries I thought I'd

---

1   Arthur M. Schlesinger Jr., *Crisis of the Old Order* (1957): p. ix.

start my career in — were already well on their way to turning inside-out, and it didn't take much imagination to sense they were mere harbingers of things to come.

It wasn't that I didn't approve of change. Exactly the opposite: I *loved* imagining the emerging possibilities. I went looking for the larger narrative for the sake of anticipating and affecting what would happen next. It was by thinking about our future that I learned to think through history.

History isn't an escape from the present, it's an attempt to identify objective reference points with which to understand the apparent chaos we're living in, either by finding events that conditioned our current situation or by finding times in which people dealt with circumstances like our own. As eloquently phrased by Jacques Barzun, one of the great historians and teachers of the 20th century, "History is formative. Its spectacle of continuity in chaos, of attainment in the heart of disorder, of purpose in the world is what nothing else provides..."[2]

The late 19th century makes a lot of sense to us now (for those of us who bother to look) but it would have looked quite different to someone living inside that historical moment — not unlike our own mixed feelings of wonder and fear in the face of "prosperity never before imagined, power never yet wielded by man, speed never reached by anything but a meteor..."[3]

We see all the specifics that made 2000 so different from 1900 and 1500 but we don't see the general shapes and tones that make those moments part of the same historical era — or rather, the similarities are obvious but they don't stand out as features, because we don't know enough about the world as it was (and might be) without them. In a few hundred years people will look back at all of these complex developments as a few simple strokes, perhaps as an extended crescendo of themes developing since the Reformation and Renaissance: individualism, secularization, abstraction, complexity, automation, arrogance...

---

2   Jacques Barzun, *Clio and the Doctors* (1974): p. 124.

3   Henry Adams, *The Education of Henry Adams* (1918,): Ch. XXXV.

We should never be too confident that old things will survive, nor too triumphant over their demise. All of our bold new ideas and institutions will eventually suffer the same fate. Today's young, self-assured dreamers and strivers (a cohort to which I belong) will grow up to be deaf and blind to changes championed by our children or grandchildren. Every generation answers at least one critical question by saying, "This time it's different." It usually precipitates a very humbling lesson.

The single most important lesson we can learn from history is this: it is too easy to forget history's lessons. Incredibly — despite how many times we're reminded by charming quotes alarming us to the risk of repeating past mistakes — we seem to keep forgetting when it counts.

Our ideas aren't necessarily wrong — but they probably are (both the old and the new). Resting with too much confidence on presumably certain ideas seems to be something we're naturally inclined to do.

While we probably can't deny this innate need for supposed certainty and narrative coherence (nor should we deny the benefits that often come with our resulting faith) it's time to grow more mature as a society — to exercise more reason and restraint, to be critical when selecting and promoting the most effective ideas while staying alert to what we might have missed.

As I came to learn more about the world I developed a sense that the answers I was looking for would never take the form of definitive statements. In the process of writing this book I realized the process was itself the answer I was looking for. We're never going to get things perfectly right — and even if we could, the fact that life keeps occurring means that unexpected events will keep occurring, which will require us to adapt our ideas and practices yet again.

We should welcome that; we should learn to enjoy the unexpected; we should learn to love the process of discovery and reconceptualization for its own sake, rather than resenting the process as a buffer between the present and our desired future.

The process is the purpose. The experience of taking steps toward attaining a goal — even if we're not perfectly sure how to articulate the ultimate aim — is what makes projects meaningful and compelling. The final products and accomplishments simply help us tell better, simpler, more effective stories. So in this sense, even "final" accomplishments aren't simply ends; they're means to continue cultivating more relevance in the world.

That's how I've conceived this book: not as the final word but as a way to tell a better story and move the conversation forward, in the most generative, open-ended, and enduring way manageable.

2 The Practice of Theory

This book developed as a loose synthesis of essays I worked on and posted online for the past couple of years. The essays have all come out of a way of thinking I carefully developed a few years ago.

It may resemble an attempt to construct a kind of grand or unified theory, but I prefer to think of it as only a set of rough sketches to keep track of what I'm doing — and to let you keep track of what I'm doing — rather than an end in itself. It's a general background for thinking more effectively about real challenges we face in this complex and dynamic age.

The problems I earnestly (and naively) started trying to solve a decade ago are the ones we read about in the paper every day: institutional dysfunction, economic volatility and inequality, environmental sustainability, demographic and geopolitical shifts, terrorism and asymmetric warfare, tensions between science and religious extremism — with consumerism in the mix — and that's just a start.

Above all I wanted to figure out why we know so little, and whether there's a better way to deal with what we don't know. Because if there's one thing we've learned in this century so far, it's that there's a lot we don't know.

One aspect of the book very roughly describes our place in history — especially the history of ideas — and suggests a specific way to understand human motivation and creativity that is more appropriate to our time. I'm trying to make some of the previous century's science somewhat more intuitive, while pragmatically addressing the challenges we face towards the future.

The second aspect of this book is an attempt to reconceive those already-existing challenges in light of this new appreciation of human nature. It isn't enough to look at the challenges themselves; I insist on also looking at *how* we look at them.

Counterintuitively, this isn't necessarily a step away from real challenges. Sometimes our old ways of looking at the world act as barriers; by stepping back to reconceive them we can find opportunities to move closer, faster towards more effective solutions.

My evidence for this is simply that I've already been applying this way of thinking to the very significant events that have occurred since 2007 and it has worked well for me. It helps me see complex challenges more clearly, which helps me communicate more effectively. The evidence is here and in the rest of my writing for you to evaluate for yourself.

That highlights the third aspect of this book: it's a *demonstration*, not simply an explanation or description of the practice of theory. The book is it's own metaphor.

As I wrote in the earlier chapter, this process of discovering and creating new ideas and conceptual frameworks is gratifying in itself. Solving problems and sharing knowledge is just something we're born to do. Like cooking, sex, competition, and music, philosophy is simply a function of human nature and there's no way to fully rationalize it. Let's just *do* it. Let's just enjoy thinking and make the most of it.

This way of approaching the world works for me, but it may not work for you, and that's fine. Other people are better suited for doing things other ways, and they're welcome to them — as long as we're nonrivalrous about it. There are a lot of opportunities to complement each other's different competencies and styles. We can't expect to be master or enjoy everything.[4]

Inclusiveness and equality of opportunity don't mean everybody can do everything they want; it means everybody has an opportunity to flourish — not just arbitrarily, but in a way that's appropriate to each individual's unique qualities and

---

4   Digitization generates very fine divisions of labour, and new metaphors for describing the networks these divisions create. I'm fond of the saying, "Do what you do best and link to the rest," by Jeff Jarvis in *What Would Google Do?* (2009): p. 26.

circumstances — yet a way that's also very richly, socially connected.

The web makes such a society more possible than ever. It was intended, and it continues to develop primarily as a framework for cultivating complex networks of relationships and defining one's own place within them.

Beyond whatever else it might be good for — and above all the complaints people have about it — social media facilitates a greater range of complementarity with a richer variety of people. There's a wide, complex range of ways to compare ourselves and interact with others. We don't have to (and shouldn't) frame our relationships in simple terms of competition or cooperation.

The web makes us more articulate — not just in the sense of being eloquent, but in the sense of clearly defining our aims, limitations, identities, and where we each fit in the narrative of our age. It compels us to cultivate a set of personal qualities that distinguish us from everyone else. As these personal impressions and brands are designed for optimizing relevance, inevitably we get better at finding ways to make ourselves desirable and useful to others, thereby adding value to society in unique ways for which we're each individually suited.

Or at least that's the hope. Of course there are valid concerns (e.g. that the Internet might also encourage social isolation, or monoculture, or both) but I think it all depends on how we use it. By merely lamenting what might be lost and fretting about the hazards, we miss opportunities to generate better outcomes. We need to focus on the benefits and ensure we're doing whatever we can to bring them to fruition.

This feeling — this hope for using the web to foster cognitive diversity — grew out of my own frustration with not sharing the same values, aims, and natural assumptions as most other people. A lot of people's skills and passions are marginalized by old social conventions and technical limitations. [5] This

---

5   See Tyler Cowen's *Create Your Own Economy* (2009), especially his case for the "hidden creativity" of people with an autistic cognitive style.

somewhat accounts for why I developed these ideas independently.

Doing this kind of work just *feels* necessary. It's just the way I am. Classifying and defining everything is just what I do. It's one of the basic rhythms of my life — like breathing. It just happens. It isn't something I have to go out and find or fabricate or fight for. I'm not driven by it or towards it; it's just one of the basic givens in my life.

While I write a lot about why intellectual stuff is so important, explaining how our society could accommodate and benefit more from it, I'm not actually advocating this for everyone. I understand (all too well) that most people aren't and won't ever be interested. I'm not trying to convince everybody. I just want to reach out to those who share my inclinations and hopefully a few others who may not exactly share this attitude but see opportunities to learn from it and teach me something in return.

It's an interesting opportunity we have now. Society has changed but we have yet to appreciate exactly how. Of course there's a lot that doesn't change — nobody doubts that — but the challenge is to figure out what that is so we can reorient our thinking back around it. To that end we find ourselves standing not just on the shoulders of giants, but also on top of mountains of data and forgotten ideas that may have been too early for their time.

The immensity of our intellectual inheritance would be impossible to fathom if we didn't also find ourselves with powerful technology for dealing with it all. The internet makes this immensity an opportunity to mine rather than a burden to carry.

That doesn't mean it will be easy. The process is going to require a lot of imagination and discipline to decouple our thinking from old assumptions.

For centuries moral philosophy was absolute. That assumption grew from religion and carried over into the scientific age. God was gradually overtaken by secular institutions, but the habit of absolutism was not.

Then society traded a spiritual religion for a mechanical one. Society itself came to be conceived as a kind of machine, in which everything could be measured, calibrated, and virtue increasingly meant maximizing efficiency.

Then through early 20th century, philosophers developed ways of thinking in morally relative terms. A lot of people started thinking and talking as if every group should be left alone to entertain their own habits and whims.

Now psychology and neuroscience are giving us better, more accountable information about what we can change and what we can't. We can use this knowledge more effectively to orient and define for ourselves what kind of person we each can and should be, to get a sense of our natural opportunities and limits.

The process of orientation goes on day-by-day as we interact with people and find where we ought to be in relation to them (and not just on one-dimensional scales like "above and below" or "ahead and behind" either). It isn't about beating others or telling them how to live; it's about understanding each other and working out ways to cultivate mutual benefits (or at least stay out of each other's way, temporarily). Life is a process of constantly growing, shaping, and integrating one's self into the most appropriate niche.

Some individuals may occupy a niche we identify as a position of leadership or control. Those are over-rated terms. Decisions are affected, and in many cases determined, by the aggregate effects in complex and dynamic networks. We could say nobody controls these networks, but we could also say *everybody* controls them. Responsibility is distributed in different degrees throughout.

Mainstream media is an especially salient demonstration of this. People complain that only a few companies control "The Media," but ultimately those companies provide what people consume and signal desire for.

However, there's also a process of conditioning, by which people learn to want specific kinds of entertainment because it's what they're familiar with.

Then again if people hadn't consented to consuming the initial offering, the decision-makers at the top would have offered something else.

And consider what some people call the obesity epidemic. The responsibility for nutrition is shared by producers and consumers alike. Of course when it comes to food we need to recognize there are chemical, biological, and psychological qualities of ingredients and advertising that producers have exploited to make consumers less able to make informed, rational decisions.

We might look to government regulation to address these problems — but I'm not sure we aren't also at risk of a regulatory epidemic as well. At some point our systems of rules could become so complicated that nobody understands the aggregate effect well enough to adapt rules to emerging circumstances. There are cases when regulation becomes a problem itself, so we need ways to address those potential challenges as well.

The best solution I can come up with — which certainly isn't a magic bullet, but I'm confident is the only way to move forward — is to regulate, but conceive regulations not as rigid boundaries, but rather as benchmarks for ongoing, open, objective, generative experiments and conversations. Everything we conceive, we should conceive as an prototype or an exercise to make our sense of judgement more effective and accountable.

This process starts with the spirit of openness — which includes an appreciation for the merits of transparency — and aspires towards the love of learning and gratification in the process itself. Culture is what matters most; if we condition appropriate attitudes and values, it will be easier to improve our regulations because more people will be willing to ask questions, manage uncertainty (rather than pretend it doesn't exist), experiment, listen, and reach out for new ideas.

As long as we perpetuate the assumption that we're trying to build the perfect system (or alternatively, that it's good enough as it already is) then we'll keep going through these crisis cycles, and that isn't good enough for me. At least this is the direction we need to move in. We'll get there eventually but we also need time to develop new skills, practices, and tools for managing it.

That's the key that a lot of people seem to neglect. For generation after generation, people's behaviour has been conditioned in economies of scarcity — often extreme scarcity, with very few day-to-day choices. Most decisions were made by authority, necessity, or habit.

Now things are different in some very important ways. We have more autonomy but we haven't learned how to manage it effectively.

Arguments that openness can't work often presume ideas about motivation based on behaviours that occurred in past conditions, which aren't necessarily valid for understanding motivation in the 21st century. It's going to take time to develop the appropriate ideas and practices for working, learning, and living in a world characterized by abundance and autonomy rather than scarcity and authority.

The big intuitive adjustment we need to make is to appreciate what really motivates people. Contrary to the assumptions that are ingrained in most of our institutions, good work (i.e. the process) is often its own reward. The notion that people will only respond to incentives may do as much harm as it does good. The examples set by open source projects like Linux, Firefox, and Wikipedia show that motivation is more nuanced than traditional economists have assumed. [6]

Looking at the big picture, society itself is a kind of open source project requiring an incomprehensible variety of skills and knowledge: planners, developers, designers, content experts, communicators, etc. Now that knowledge, information, and ideas are becoming more prominent and routine, I expect new divisions of labour will form for people who have knowledge- and idea-related skills. This is why I've invested so much time and energy in the "practice of theory" I'm demonstrating here.

---

6   I'll get into the psychology in a later chapter. From an organizational perspective I'd recommend starting with Jeffrey Pfeffer & Robert Sutton's *Hard Facts, Dangerous Half-Truths, and Total Nonsense* (2006).

There seems to be deeply ingrained skepticism than anyone can start to make sense of the big picture. It might be because it's almost as difficult to trust someone who *claims* to have a sense of the big picture as it is for people to appreciate it themselves.

It may also have a lot to do with the way our old institutions act as barriers to information. If all of the most important knowledge and data is owned and guarded by specific parties, then generalists and synthesizers never have a chance to demonstrate the potential for new uses. Fortunately the Internet is creating both the opportunity and the need for us to demonstrate these new practices and prove it's possible to something out of everything.

Society needs thinkers to conduct ongoing conversations about the relative merits and risks of various ideas and practices without going so far as to presume we're smart enough to know the right answers (or even wrap our heads around the whole picture at once). The role of rational intellect isn't to judge and decide; it's rather to point out similarities and differences among things, to ask questions, to challenge assumptions, to outline new possibilities that might be investigated — in short, to criticize and keep the learning process alive.

These open, conceptual practices are especially important for appreciating the most general aspects of society, for which nobody with a specific job title is technically accountable for. Think this way about the big, general categories of enterprise: science, business, art, media, technology, and civics. We need to make the aims and methods in each of these domains open and articulate so we have the means to gradually tie (and untie) their narratives in relation to each other.

We need to engage both of life's two essential aspects — hard and soft, spatial and temporal, static and dynamic — through these processes. The purpose of what's persistent is to direct what flows, while the purpose of what flows is to form and flex what's persistent.

Conversations ensue about how we should live according to our various natures, what kind of values and rules and norms we ought to follow — and maybe for the sake of discussion, some of it presumes to be absolute and universal. It isn't exactly wrong to make that presumption, as long as we understand it's just a provisional heuristic — something that will have to do for now — while staying open to better alternatives.

Maybe most people will never participate directly in this aspect of the conversation, and we'll probably never settle on a set of ideas that are suitable for all. But agreement on a single set of rules isn't the point. The point is that by thinking and talking about them — while other people live and work in their own unique ways — we're already doing what makes our lives meaningful, productive, and fun. Reconciling, enriching, and perpetuating our personal stories *is* the purpose of life.

The conversation we have about ideas, moral values, and social aims is analogous to what life is all about on a more general level: interacting with others, figuring out where to place each other in the most effective, meaningful, and relevant ways.

3 Common Aspirations

In August 2007 the financial world began a period of decline from which it has yet to pull out of. According to economic indicators there has been recent growth, but culturally and intellectually the industry continues to be affl icted by distrust. Prominent economists call it a crisis of understanding.[7] Basic assumptions are just beginning to change. There's no reason to believe the root causes have been addressed, and people know it.

In the U.S., trust in the system is diminishing from both the right and the left. There has reportedly been a spike in sales of Ayn Rand's *Atlas Shrugged*, a book depicting widespread withdrawal from society by the most productive citizens in response to excessive central control. It doesn't take a big stretch of the imagination to be reminded of the anti-tax Tea Party protests. As with the anti-prorogation rallies held across Canada, the way in which they were loosely organized across the new media landscape with relatively little planning and control is almost as fascinating — and maybe more demonstrative — than their espoused message.

To me the financial crisis hasn't merely been a problem in itself but rather a symptom of an inadequate understanding of human nature and the thin system of values that goes with it. It's time to update that. The old ideas worked well enough in a more industrialized society, but that kind of society and the ideas that came with it evolved to address the challenges and opportunities of a different age. Industrialism has created another whole set of challenges and opportunities in its wake; we need to imagine new conceptual frameworks for addressing them — just as people once imagined the frameworks we've used until now.

---

7   "A Crisis of Understanding" by Robert Shiller at project-syndicate.org (March 12, 2010).

Think of two general patterns of change occurring. One is that we've been shifting from an economy defined in terms of scarcity to an economy defined in terms of abundance. The other pattern is that we're shifting from a society organized around authority to a society organized around individual autonomy. These don't apply to every aspect of life, but they are having a profound affect on how we work, learn, and live.

But abundance and autonomy can't be taken for granted. They aren't simply given to us; we actively generate and sustain them. It requires effort and ingenuity. It's a big, social learning experience, which we have to keep re-investing our attention and energy back into. With the wrong cultural mindset, we might repeatedly gravitate back to authoritarianism and scarcity. This book is an effort to reconceive assumptions that might threaten to turn progress into regression, or worse. Specifically, this book focuses on personal autonomy (others can focus on abundance).

People have probably never had as much freedom to decide what to do with each moment of our lives as we do now,[8] but we're still using assumptions and conventions inherited from closed societies in which occupations were far more limited, far more determined. In other words, we haven't learned how to use our freedom. Our decisions are mostly made by necessity or by authority — or the authority of popularity. We've earned autonomy but we haven't *learned* autonomy yet; we only know how to follow. Even most of our leaders tend to follow conventions and mere whims of the group.

It's especially important that we learn because we've also become interconnected in more complex ways, and we're leaving lasting digital impressions through our choices. Our decisions have immediate effects we may not be aware of. Look at how memes spread online; look at how our choices are framed by whatever has been most popular in the past — whatever induced the most people to click, whatever fits the user profile you conditioned through previous behaviours, purchases, remarks, etc.

---

8   See Clay Shirky's talk on "Gin, Television, and Cognitive Surplus": http://www.edge.org/3rd_culture/shirky08/shirky08_index.html

It isn't just about choices we make online. Look at market rallies and panics that are affected more by what everyone else is doing than any objective, non-psychological factors.

Our thinking in too many areas has become untethered from all sense of objective value other than that of money. In the past, decisions were largely guided by necessity, habit, and authority. People did things because they had to, or they were told to, or because they couldn't imagine any alternatives.

Religion provided the conceptual frameworks for most societies in the past. Regardless of whether there was a formal distinction between church and state a century ago, individual decisions were more likely to have been affected by principles and values associated with religious belief — shared, enduring principles and values — rather than just the unstable cross-currents of high-turnover social trends, a prevalent attitude of personal entitlement,[9] and endless desire.

What we need are better ways to frame opportunities and direct our own will, our own attention, our own sense of autonomy, our own decisions, so the risks are more apparent, and so more of us can get better at making these frames by asking better questions and approaching decisions as learning experiences.

To me it seems like the shift in mindset reaches all the way to the attitude we have towards achievement. This notion registered with me after I read an interesting article about the risk marathons run of being ruined by their own success. A few decades ago marathon running was an obscure activity, now marathons are astonishingly popular, and potentially face the problem of too many people wanting to participate.[10]

It made me wonder if that's maybe representative of more general hazards we risk running into by promoting the importance of being so aggressively "goal-driven" and

---

9   Jean Twenge's *Generation Me* (2006) is a good place to start, and Christopher Lasch's *Culture of Narcissism* (1979) is a good reminder that Generation Y didn't invent self-absorption.

10   "Big Marathons, Already Packed, May Still Grow," by Juliet Macur for the *New York Times* (October 28, 2008):

conceiving one's life as a series of competitive accomplishments.

Some people might wonder, "How could there be any other kind of life?" The goal-driven life is such an essential characteristic of our age that we assume it could never have been otherwise — but who had time for so many "goals" two or three generations ago?

Sure, people in past generations and ages certainly wanted to accomplish things, they had aims and ambitions, but they weren't going after them as deliberately (or arbitrarily), or with such variety as we do today — and they didn't have as many alternatives either.

While there are plenty of people who run marathons who simply must run marathons, there are also people for whom running a marathon is on a list of a whole bunch of things they want to accomplish at some point (along with perhaps, getting a graduate degree, learning to play guitar, seeing the pyramids, climbing a mountain, writing a book, retiring early, learning another language).

While I was writing this I found an interesting blog post by Robin Hanson about "wanting to want" — for example, wanting to be attracted to intelligence, talking about being attracted to intelligence, but actually being attracted to looks: "We want what is useful to us, but we want to want what makes us look good to others. We often fool ourselves into thinking that what we want to want is what we do want, and thereby also often fool others into thinking well of us." [11]

What most people actually want are ambiguous qualities like respect, belonging, and security. It's difficult for each of us to know what our true ambition is. It's so deep that we may not be able to see or articulate it. Maybe running marathons, earning degrees, and writing books tend to be ways in which we try to understand, define, and express our true ambition through trial and error. In this sense, goals are reference points [12]

---

11 Robin Hanson, "Wanting to Want," overcomingbias.com (October 28, 2008).

12 Background via Chip Heath, Richard Larrick & George Wu, "Goals as

— the means by which we assess our own aspirations; trying to achieve a goal is the way to find out how worth-while it is — and a way to learn how to choose the next set of goals.

Thinking about this some more, these goals aren't about wanting to want, they're about *having* to want — people have to want accomplishments in order to build successful careers and enjoy fulfilling lives. Pursuing goals as a lifestyle is no less (or more) valid than my lifestyle of pursuing truth.

The achievement-centric society has accomplished a lot of great things (and for a lot of people, pursuing goals is as much like breathing as pursuing knowledge is for me), but I worry that we might be reaching a point not just of diminishing returns, but irreparable damage — like bodybuilders pumping themeless with steroids or financial engineers pumping their companies with sophisticated instruments. My worry is that this achievement-centric culture has taken over a lot of areas that were once largely occupied by people who took genuine pride in doing a job well for its own sake, and now we're losing a lot of the quality and generative, sustainable, socially shared value that came from that.[13]

Higher education is full of people who are obliged to get bachelor's degrees they don't actually want or theoretically need. It has more to do with administrative expedience and accountability than learning: enough people have degrees that hiring managers can make it a minimum requirement, and as it becomes a requirement for more jobs, more people get degrees, and on it goes.

At an even higher level, I take it that it isn't sufficient that university professors be excellent teachers, passionate about their subject; one must maintain a steady cadence of published articles, grants, patents, etc — accomplishments — I fear at the expense of more generative kinds of work, more open-ended research, and more effective teaching.

An easy response to my complaints might be to cite research

Reference Points," *Cognitive Psychology*, 38 (1999): p. 79 - 109.

13 On this point, Richard Sennett's *Culture of the New Capitalism* (2006) and Charles Taylor's *Malaise of Modernity* (1991) are especially poignant.

showing that goals tend to make people happier, more, successful, more gratified, etc. Sure, but people also have to live within a society, and if the society fails, happiness and success will be harder for *every*one to find.

What if the aggregate effect of so much "accomplishment" is that we wreck our society by channelling too many people towards accomplishments they didn't really want or need? Maybe the problem comes down to a "paradox of choice": with too much to choose from, we can't effectively choose at all — or at least we won't be satisfied by any particular choice for very long.[14] No matter what we choose, almost everyone we meet will have something better. So we tend to follow the crowd — rushing from bubble-to-bubble looking for the most sought-after trophies.

Call it a superbubble — the Goal Bubble. Our society has spent more time and energy on trophies that are totally dependent on demand than on stuff that generates and sustains value independently. The financial devastation we've witnessed is nothing compared to the intellectual, aesthetic, and moral devastation that might yet occur.

It's wasteful if people do things like going back to school for a graduate degree in a subject they don't especially care about in order to jump up into a higher pay grade in an organization that makes them miserable. Not everybody wants a PhD, but a lot of people want to be perceived as the type of person who does, or the type of person who can accomplish that. A lot of people run marathons because they want to be perceived as someone who wants that accomplishment. Maybe everyone really wants something else, but everyone's been so preoccupied trying to play the market.

Not only does this potentially burden the individual overachiever's future by placing them on a treadmill of desired accomplishments, but at some point it starts to diminish the value in those experiences for the people who genuinely need to run marathons or need to be involved in research. They start to find there are too many elbows in the way, too many people

14 Barry Schwartz, *Paradox of Choice* (2004).

competing for these accomplishments, and the field begins to favour those who approach it as a game — something to be won and marked as an accomplishment before moving on to the next on the list.

One might argue that that's reality — that's the way things are done, that's what career is all about... And that's precisely the problem. It's the attitude that inflates the superbubble of wanting to want.

Wanting to want is profitable only as long as everyone else wants to want too. Once everyone else in the market starts figuring out that their life isn't really improved by the endless race for ever-greater accomplishments, and people start looking for qualitative value and meaning by turning away from objective trophies, then our whole framework of assumptions about career and "success" based on other people's dreams could start to collapse.

Again, this cultural attitude has accomplished a lot, but I interpret events like the financial crisis and its related symptoms (the flood of talent into financial fields[15] and astronomical pay for the few highest performers — which isn't connected to their firm's long-term performance — and "ordinary people" taking on too much risk in the hope of financial freedom) as signs that there is a point at which it can't progress without a fundamental reset. [16]

For me the recovery won't occur until we've mastered new ideas and practices for exercising personal autonomy — beginning with our conceptions of motivation.

For decades, our education system and institutions have assumed that goals and incentives are the *only* way to motivate and reward people. From the first day of school people are taught one thing above all: how to learn by being taught rather than taking the initiative and learning for one's self.

---

15 "Flocking to Finance," *Harvard Crimson* (May-June 2008).

16 As far as I know, the "reset" concept started with Jeffrey Immelt at the Business for Social Responsibility Conference in New York (November 6, 2008). Kurt Anderson and Richard Florida have written books on the theme: *Reset* (2009) and *The Great Reset* (2010) respectively.

Until we start educating people to make their own decisions, to recognize problems and opportunities that emerge from outside (or in between, or up from below) existing institutional frameworks — i.e. caring about more than "what's on the test" or what achievements time-constrained recruiters are looking for than genuine learning — then we won't begin to address the root human conditions at the core of the global economic crisis.

In other words, we need to start loving learning and making things because it's rewarding in itself — *not instead of* being goal-driven, *but as well as* being goal-driven. It isn't about one approach or the other, it's about finding and regulating a sustainable balance.

We can still have goals, we can still run marathons (maybe I will some day), we can still compete vigourously for promotions — and I certainly appreciate there are people for whom goals and accomplishments are as essential as discovery and innovation are to me — but we need to appreciate that the goals aren't inherently good, it's the *process* of attaining them that we find so gratifying.

And with that understanding we can talk about the kinds of nonrivalrous accomplishments that scale and can be shared in common — possessions like knowledge, by which we can enable rather than exclude others — and with those, we improve our ability to identify and define goals that are better, more generative investments for us over the long term.

4 A New Lightning Rod

In terms of understanding motivation and the creative process, the stage we're at now seems a lot like people's knowledge of electricity in the mid-18th century.

We have plenty of excellent research but no "lightning rod" to capture and conduct our imaginations — no easy way to accurately intuit how motivation and creativity work. We're just starting to truly capture and conduct it. Most of our common intuitions still struggle via older models, and there's no focal concept as to what creativity is, exactly.

Many people and organizations have a very good knack for motivation and creativity, but they seem to have acquired it by luck and dogged persistence through trial and error rather than explicit understanding. We talk about it a lot, sharing many good observations, platitudes, and techniques, but it still eludes a really precise explanation.

Similarly, consider that before Benjamin Franklin's famous kite experiment, "electricians" had developed a lot of tricks for generating sparks, storing charges in jars, and conducting mild shocks through groups of people holding hands, but there was little agreement as to what electricity was and how to proceed with further investigations.[17]

As lightning tore through buildings and struck people dead, its seemingly bizarre leaps and turns were explained as the will of God. Ironically, people tried to ward off storms by ringing church bells — which didn't work for reasons we know well. A lot of bell-ringers died, and even after Franklin's findings were publicized bells were still being made bearing engravings that memorialized their misguided and often deadly purpose.[18]

---

17 On scientific paradigms, using Franklin's work as an example, see Thomas Kuhn's Structure *of Scientific Revolutions*, (1962): p. 14 - 15.

18 The contextual information is from Philip Dray's *Stealing God's Thunder: Benjamin Franklin's Lightning Rod and the Invention of America* (2005)

This seems to be where we're at with human nature. Our ideas and practices work sometimes; other times they don't — and I'm not sure things work out *because* of our attempts to manage motivation and creativity or *despite* those attempts. I don't mean to diminish the merits of some very creative organizations and admirable initiatives, but looking at humanity with a wider lens, it looks like we're missing something essential.

Think about some of the questions we've been dealing with in the 21st century: What do we do about suicide bombers? What do we do about corporate corruption? What do we do about poverty? What do we do about market irrationality that has recently come very close to undermining the whole global economy? How do we negotiate fair agreements on climate change and trade? What do we do about abuses of intellectual property law? How can we help developing countries without counterproductively being perceived as trying to meddle with and exploit them? How do we resolve moral and ethical dilemmas in science?

Many of our responses to those questions look to me a lot like ringing church bells in a lightning storm. They often have results that are precisely opposed to what we want, but we keep doing it anyway for lack of any viable alternatives, perpetuating our false intuitions with intellectually lazy determination to *do something dammit!*

If someone commits violence against us we commit right back — which begets more violence in return. We fight corporate corruption and volatile markets by making more rules; more rules make people less morally responsible and they become even more determined and adept at exploiting more sophisticated rules. We hand out money to the poor and it often further diminishes their ability and will to support themselves. We try to persuade others to adopt our practices and beliefs and it makes them even more steadfast in theirs — and vice versa.[19]

---

19 My concerns are corroborated by the recent wave of popular books about irrationality, especially associated with behavioural economics: Cass Sunstein and Richard Thaler's *Nudge* (2008), Robert Shiller and George

Somewhere in all of this we must be missing some essential insight that will seem obvious to people a century or two from now. Where can we look for ideas to guide us a little more effectively? What's our lightning rod for creativity and motivation?

Akerlof's *Animal Spirits* (2009), Dan Ariely's *Predictably Irrational* (2008), and *Sway* by Ori and Rom Brafman (2008).

5 The Web as a Way of Understanding

Our tools, activities and surroundings literally teach us how to think.[20] We constantly absorb metaphors and images that go on to inform our intuition and reason.[21]

As life and work get more networked and dynamic via the Web, our online activities also provide new metaphors for making sense of the emerging structures and systems. The web is becoming a better model for understanding older aspects of the world, which still baffle us — complex aspects like motivation, creativity, and consciousness.

Demonstrating my point best is the concept of "memes." Seven or eight years ago the term was nonsensical to most people I knew. Unless you had read Richard Dawkins[22] you probably would have raised an eyebrow at the suggestion that ideas are like genes, selected and reproduced through culture, using us as carriers to maintain their own survival. But then Digg , YouTube, Twitter and the rest came along, and suddenly the idea makes intuitive sense to an entire generation with barely any explanation at all.

Now, not only is "meme" a mainstream concept, but people are using the concept to make more platforms and applications that work on that same principle. With these newer applications we'll gain more elaborate metaphors and models from those, and so on. Further, these apps are fertile ground for research by anthropologists, sociologists, psychologists, and other social

---

20 See *Einstein's Clocks, Poincaré's Maps* (2003) by Peter Galison for a sense of how 20th century science was affected by 19th century technology, e.g. via Einstein's experience working in the patent office.

21 See George Lakoff & Mark Johnson's *Metaphors We Live By* (1980). For something more recent and comprehensive read Steven Pinker's *Stuff of Thought* (2007).

22 Richard Dawkins, *The Selfish Gene* (1976).

scientists.[23] The Web generates massive amounts of hard data. More to the point, it's data that's already digitized for analysis and visualization. We can use it in many more effective ways, and it doesn't have to be manually entered into a new system for each specific use.

Beyond that, as we already know, the knowledge that may result from all that research can be more readily accessed by anybody, as it's more easily searchable and there's a corresponding trend towards open access journals and other alternatives to conventional publishing.

And it isn't just today's research we're gaining more access to; we're also getting close to the entire history of human knowledge, right at our fingertips. After all, data doesn't tell the whole story; sometimes it prevents us from seeing the forest for the trees. Taking a step back to see what people thought and wrote about human fundamentals 100 years ago, 200 years ago, 2000 years ago (because some things will never change) can be very fruitful, if not essential.

And there's one more factor we can't forget: it isn't just the data and ideas that are connected, *we're* connected. Better ways to converse and collaborate bring the other three developments together even more richly, making the possibilities for learning literally unimaginable. The World Wide Web was always intended to be a platform for connecting knowledge and ideas by connecting people.[24]

This awesome new way to work and learn puts us in a world of abundance and autonomy that compels us to create ambitious new ideas and practices. Thinking of Clay Shirky's well known claim that "we are living in the middle of the largest increase of expressive capability in the history of the human race,"[25] I have to wonder exactly what it is we're all expressing. My hope is

---

23 Much of the research that went into Nicholas Christakis and James Fowler's recent book about the effects of social networks, *Connected* (2009), was done on Facebook.

24 Tim Berners-Lee, *Weaving the Web* (1999),

25 Clay Shirky, *Here Comes Everybody* (2008): p. 106.

that we're also in one of the most profound philosophical transformations as well. The Web is helping create a culture in which we're comfortable working, learning, and living in real-time; we're "abandoning stocks to embrace flows";[26] we're learning to think in beta, improving the process rather than hopelessly trying to perfect every product.[27]

It will all keep improving, as long as we keep making it better. Like any technology, the Internet can be abused. It can be wasteful, misleading — even dangerous. It's also the best tool we have for navigating this historical transition we're living through. Our understanding, like the Web and everything else, is a work in progress.

---

26 John Hagel, John Seely Brown, and Lang Davison, "Abandon Stocks, Embrace Flows," HBR Blogs (January 27, 2009): http://blogs.hbr.org/bigshift/2009/01/abandon-stocks-embrace-flows.html

27 Jeff Jarvis, "Product v. process journalism: The myth of perfection v. beta culture," at buzzmachine.com (June 7, 2009).

6 Uncertainty & Spatial Bias

It's natural to try identifying a particular object as being *the* cause of something. We want to nail it down and say, "*here's* the cause, right here; just fix this and we're all good," or, "*here's* what makes us conscious... and *here's* what set the universe in motion: the mystery is *solved* once and for all!"

Yet, again and again, all of the causes we identify — causes of failure, causes of wars, causes of great accomplishments, causes of natural and physical facts — keep pointing even farther and farther back.

At some point making sense of these complex systems gets too difficult. Inevitably in every investigation we stop tracing causal chains back in time and we start looking at general patterns (sometimes imagined ones) and then we give the pattern a name like good, evil, hate, love, greed, resentment, altruism, change, uncertainty, chance, or something else abstract. It's unavoidable. Sometimes it works pretty well; other times it doesn't.

Saying that evil "caused" 9/11 and greed "caused" numerous financial breakdowns doesn't explain anything. They're simply names we give patterns of social phenomena. When we say "greed caused the financial crisis" we're simply saying people's behaviour through the financial crisis is consistent with behaviour we conveniently tend to categorize as "greedy."

It's the individual *events* that are responsible, not the categories we use to make sense of them. Yet we have to act on the ideas we have, so we accept them and get on with it — however imperfect they may be — at least until we can come up with better explanations.

But then we're still left with questions about the causes of behaviour that's greedy, altruistic, etc. These ought to be left to specialized researchers to answer scientifically. Unfortunately we can't afford to wait for their answers. Political and economic questions need to be addressed with the best knowledge we have *now*. We have to proceed with the imperfect knowledge we have.

And we *want* to proceed with our imperfect knowledge. Whether one tends to take action or tends to reflect on ideas, we can't stop ourselves from believing *some*thing. There's never a moment you're not doing or making things, and we're constantly experiencing various feeling of attraction and revulsion, desire and disgust. And then there are even more basic processes we take for granted.

Things are always happening. Right now we're both breathing, our hearts are pumping oxygen from our lungs to our brains, making sure our neurons fire fast enough to translate the light hitting our eyes into images and words, affecting our streams of thought and influencing our ideas.

Even when we die there are processes of decay occurring. Meanwhile the planet moves in orbit while the burning sun evaporates rivers and seas which condenses into clouds that are blown by winds until changing temperatures release rain that falls to fill reservoirs and streams and nourish the plants that generate the oxygen that circulates to our brains so we can think about these things.

Think of a whirlpool that forms over a drain and persists as long as water continues to flow into it. Now think of the same sort of motion occurring in a hurricane seen from Space, or the Great Red Spot seen on Jupiter's surface.[28] We think and talk about these stable, nonequilibrium ordered systems as if they are permanent, discrete objects — as if they could exist independently — but their existence depends on ongoing *occurrences*: energy and matter flowing both into and out of them.

Such nonequilibrium ordered systems, called "dissipative structures," are very common in our world. Ilya Prigogine was awarded the 1977 Nobel Prize in Chemistry for his research on

---

28 Stuart Kaufman, *At Home in the Universe* (1995): p. 20 - 21.

these dynamic systems, and spent much of the rest of his life urging the broader scientific community to appreciate temporal characteristics.[29]

Temporality is tough to fully appreciate because we usually take time for granted. We evolved to go with the flow while building structures and tools from all the blocks and bits of hard stuff around us. We evolved to perceive and shape the rigid outlines of objects while ignoring the ambiguous flux that's constantly occurring — not just around us, but in us (and *as* us) as well.

Most of what we take for granted in our social and economic realities are either dissipative structures or affected (i.e. within) dissipative structures; we can talk about them as if they're solid things, but their existence depends on continuous *occurrence*. For example, if every economic indicator hypothetically stayed flat for a year, it would not be because everything stopped, it would be because of constant production, revenues keeping up with expenditures, steady turnover of employment, etc. Likewise, even the proverbial small town where "nothing ever happens" and the population stays the same actually consists of many complementary occurrences — like the rhythms of the seasons or the human body.

Even *you and I* are nonequilibrium systems, composed of — and suspended by — multiple dissipative structures: the cells in our bodies are nonequilibrium systems exchanging matter and energy with surrounding structures, our thoughts are nonequilibrium systems; so are our communities, our organizations, and our economies. If it wasn't for events constantly occurring through and around us, we wouldn't exist at all — and if we could exist (absurdly) without occurrence, it would be at the expense of action, sensation, mind, or any future whatsoever.

These processes are so constant, they're so established, so regular, we hardly even think of them as happening. We conveniently conceptualize all these living processes as static things. We describe these processes as collections of parts —

---

29 E.g. in Prigogine's widely available *End of Certainty* (1997).

like parts of a car that can be kept on cognitive shelves in our minds and our books until we need to assemble them, one-by-one, into theories.

Like the poet said,

> Our meddling intellect
> Mis-shapes the beauteous forms of things:--
> We murder to dissect. [30]

Then we find ourselves stuck with static models that don't move and grow the way things do in real life, so we have to ask, "What makes all of these processes go?" — "What is life?" "What is altruism?" "What is time?" — and we roll up our sleeves, carving away, looking for the force or particle that animates the world.

But we're looking for the wrong things. We shouldn't be looking for any *thing* at all. Instead we should recognize that by conceptualizing life as an assemblage of static parts we've omitted, or "murdered" and sterilized the simple fact that things *always happen*, and the notion that things can exist without happening is just a hypothetical construct that is often useful but can't always be exploited.

To get a better sense this bias and what's required to counter it, try to imagine the smallest particles of matter. If you're like me, you probably start by visualizing spatial forms that are absolutely sterilized of temporal qualities, and *then* you hit the proverbial ON switch to set them in motion. There is no empirical or rational justifi cation for thinking like this, unless we're thinking about machines and other things we fabricate ourselves. Everything that occurs in nature (including your own mind) has both spatial and temporal characteristics; there's no way to know which came first.

If we allow ourselves to imagine purely spatial objects despite the fact we know that everything has temporal characteristics, what happens if we try the contrasting approach? Try imagining the smallest particles of matter by conceptualizing

---

30 William Wordsworth, "The Tables Turned; An Evening Scene, on the Same Subject" (1798).

purely temporal characteristics first, and then give them spatial form... I'm not sure it's possible to start. I can't even imagine a "purely temporal characteristic" without first imagining spatial forms.

For heuristic purposes, if we imagine a spectrum between pure space and pure time (while noting how we rely on another spatial image to do so), motion and becoming would be in the *middle* of that spectrum; they aren't directly opposed to rest (or fixity) and being. Motion and becoming involve both time *and* space, while fixity and being are abstractions at the extreme end of pure space. Timelines and ticking clocks would be in the middle of the spectrum too — those have spatial characteristics.

It's kind of an absurd exercise — but also an enlightening one, which vividly demonstrates that, as Henri Bergson put it, "intellectualized time is space... the elimination of time is the habitual, normal, commonplace act of our understanding." [31]

Specifically, I call this "spatial bias": our tendency to frame concepts in spatial terms, thereby diminishing the importance of life's temporal qualities. Spatial bias is what leads us to make categories and taxonomies — often very useful ones, but sometimes perniciously for their own sake. Spatial bias is what leads us to treat some categories and abstractions as if they are real things that have actual effects in the world, other than conceptual ones. [32]

When we try to understand something affected by complex processes (e.g. consciousness, motivation, creativity, and evolution), there's a tendency to spend a lot of cognitive energy asking broad questions about *Why?*, *How?*, and *What is...?* Often such questions are unanswerable — at least until better information or more penetrating insight is available. In such cases, let's just say *things happen because time exists* so we can focus on moving forward and dealing with real, practical, nitty gritty details.

---

31 See *The Creative Mind*, tr. Mabelle L. Andison (1946): p. 19.

32 This specific fallacy is called reification. Also see Whitehead's notion of the "fallacy of misplaced concreteness" in *Science in the Modern World* (1925, 1997): p. 51.

This is roughly what Bergson suggested a century ago: "time is what is happening, and more than that, it is what causes everything to happen."[33] It's a deliberately open way of accounting for "the very mobility of being"[34] — or the fact that everything in life (down to the smallest particle) seems constantly motivated to assert itself.

It's important not to interpret this "vital principle" as a postulation of some kind of cosmic force, substance, or thing; it's precisely the opposite: it's a kind of heuristic placeholder we can use to prevent false ideas from settling before better information is available. As Bergson wrote, it which "may indeed not explain much, but it is at least a sort of label affixed to our ignorance, so as to remind us of this occasionally."[35]

It's through our dispositions represented by spatial bias that both materialism and vitalism have been corrupted into ungrounded abstractions. Materialism often degenerates into a belief that everything *must* be reduced to static fossils and chalkboard diagrams — as if we could see altruism under a microscope, or cut greed out with a scalpel. Vitalism often degenerates into a belief that there's some kind of spirit pushing and pulling everything behind the scenes.

Note that the word "bias" doesn't imply that its effects are *necessarily* negative. If it wasn't for our tendency to conceive objects and patterns as permanent — even when we can't see them (starting with Mommy or Daddy playing peak-a-boo behind a blanket) — then we wouldn't have geometry, math, or even an alphabet to work with. On a more complex level, without spatial bias we wouldn't have science, religion, commerce, or legal systems. All of these require a sense that structural and patternistic abstractions are really concrete and permanent.

My point is that we should *know the limitations and distortions* conditioned by that practice and be open to alternatives when trying to understand new challenges and complex

---

33 *The Creative Mind*, tr. Mabelle L Andison (1946): p. 2.

34 *Creative Evolution*, tr. Arthur Mitchell (1911): p. 366.

35 *Creative Evolution*, tr. Arthur Mitchell (1911): p. 48.

processes (e.g. consciousness, motivation, creativity, perceptions of meaning, love).

This is more important now than ever, as we try to understand a hyper-connected world in which global events play out in real-time. We can't assume anything is fixed anymore.

Again, as I suggested at the start of this chapter, I trust scientific experts to figure everything out *eventually*, but in the mean time we have some severe challenges that aren't going to wait, and a lot of impatient idealists proposing solutions that may cause more problems and delays than they solve — cowering under the spectre of evil and shouting down mere caricatures of greed rather than addressing real, complex behaviours and their root causes.

By balancing spatialized concepts with an equally, deliberately fallacious notion that things are "caused" by the "existence" of time (I'll call it the "temporalist maxim"), I'm trying to maintain the benefits we get from purely spatial assumptions while accounting for inevitably uncertain and random occurrences. Like Bergson, I use this as "a sort of label affixed to our ignorance."

Note that science already does this. Think of notions like "uncertainty" and "chance," without which we wouldn't have good understandings of quantum physics or evolution. The notion that "things happen because time exists" is essentially a generalization of those notions. It's useful for balancing our spatial metaphors and descriptions, as well as neutralizing, and postponing the need to identify specific, over-simplistic, erroneously fixed causes.

Above all, the "temporalist maxim" helps keep explanations open to new insights for appreciating the dynamic and complex conditions that constantly reshape our world. We can say the more precisely we've described what something *is* in spatial terms, the less we know about what it's going to *do;* likewise, the more tacitly we appreciate what's happening, the more we should expect we'll need to articulate in concrete terms.

7 Will to Relevance

At no waking moment do the streams of thought and feeling stop flowing in our minds. There's always *some*thing happening. We're constantly considering ways to affect our surroundings, we continuously conceive a sense of our future selves, and we're always imagining actions that might make those thoughts reality.

There doesn't have to be a specific purpose to these thoughts; they may simply occur *because we can't stop* thinking and feeling, so we must think and feel *some*thing.

When a single idea seems to stick in one's mind, it isn't just sitting there like an inert stone (and even a stone doesn't just sit, but is held by an equilibrium of forces). Persistent and "stable" ideas are actually refreshed and held in place by thoughts streaming around. Even meditating "on nothing" is not a cessation of thinking but rather a channelling of consciousness into recurrent and regulated patterns (e.g. by focusing on the breath).

As discussed in the previous chapter, the fact that we tend to think of ideas as concrete, fixed objects is due more to cognitive bias than any real evidence. This essay is an attempt to correct, or overcome those — to think about thinking, knowledge, creativity, and motivation more effectively.

In itself, thinking can be a way to experience a sense of efficacy and relevance — specifically when opportunities in the physical environment aren't as accessible or fruitful, i.e. when there is nothing around to act on, or when circumstances are too difficult to engage in, or when some insight has just occurred that generates thoughts that are more compelling than what's happening in the real world.

On another level, there seems to be a natural tendency for people to interpret events as being more relevant to one's self than what might actually be the case (especially if outcomes are positive).

Such "self-centredness" is understandable, given that we're each irremovably placed, essentially, at the centre of our own unique world (or frame, or horizon, or whatever you want to call it). Most of what you experience *does* have something to do with you because you're the one factor that's *constantly there.* You're the "usual suspect" who happens to be at the scene of virtually every event you experience.

But we learn to appreciate that even though we happen to always be at the centre of everything we experience, our world isn't there *because* of us, or for our sake. We understand that things happen for other reasons, which don't necessarily relate to us; but there are still other biases preventing us from making our explanations completely accurate. Factors like availability, salience, and vividness are what determine our immediate explanations (which isn't to say we can't learn to generate more objective patterns of thought that happen to be just as available, salient, and vivid as subjective ones). [36]

Conventional models of motivation and choice don't handle these facts very well. This is where the Web as a metaphor becomes more useful. Specifically I use the concept of *relevance* — emphasizing the connotations coming from Google's use of "relevance" as their scale for ranking web pages — as a metaphor for the connections we make and the meanings we derive from them.

Socially, commercially, and intellectually we constantly construct webs of connections through our lives, trying to place ourselves where the connections have the greatest continued effect, but the results or reasons for our connections are secondary — not ends-in-themselves, but rather means — to forming relationships with and among people, objects, and ideas, the process of which is purposeful in itself.

It's as if we're motivated by a kind of "will to relevance" that compels us to pursue the most meaningful relationships. Even placing ourselves in a position of contrast, tension, competition, dominance, and submission is a way of being

---

36 The academic book to read is *Judgement Under Uncertainty: Heuristics and Biases* (1982), by Daniel Kahneman, Paul Slovic, and Amos Tversky.

conceptually or cognitively relevant — though perhaps not the most effective way (in the same way that electricity will fl ow through poor conductors, if poor conductors are the only means available for conduction).

The concept of will to relevance was the answer to a problem that had obsessed me on and off since my early high school years: *What motivates us? Why do we do what we do? What makes us happy?* I didn't just want an inventory of various hungers and drives; I wanted to know *the* secret of human nature.

A second year university course pointed me to Nietzsche and his concept of "will to power."[37] For several years I referred back to that as a provisional solution — but not one that was ultimately satisfying.

Maybe I wasn't satisfied because I didn't fully grasp Nietzsche's meaning (I'm not sure I do now, even). I tended to conceive it with excessive overtones of Hobbes and Machiavelli, who themselves had also been simplified by interpreting statements like "warre of every man against every man"[38] too narrowly. I literally took "power" to mean *objective* power over people and things. Altruism was thus conceived as a "selfish" (and self-deceptive) kind of act with a selfi sh purpose (i.e. I wondered if good deeds are performed in order to feel superior to others, or to make others indebted for future benefits).

I was never totally confident about that "selfish" formulation of human nature, but I also wasn't comfortable rejecting (or even ignoring) it merely because it was unpleasantly cynical. I was still very much open to the possibility that people gain *some*thing by being altruistic; I refused to accept the blindly optimistic fantasy that some people are often just nice and good (while others are just evil) without asking questions — as if no explanation would be needed or even wanted.

As my thinking matured (and as I actually read more of Nietzsche and tried to understand what he wrote, rather than

---

37 See Nietzsche's *Beyond Good & Evil,* especially sections 13 & 36.
38 Thomas Hobbes, *Leviathan* (1651, 1985 Penguin): p. 185.

just adorning my thoughts with misappropriated Nietzschean slogans), I began to rely less on over-simple dichotomies (like good-evil, selfish-unselfish); I started my own attempt at a "revaluation of all values" aimed at getting "beyond good & evil."

The problem with the simplified good-evil accounts of human nature is that they ignore much of life's temporal aspect. They treat people as hard, fixed, well-defined mechanical units, and once we conceptualize people this way, we feel compelled to attribute inherent, permanent qualities. But our behaviour is affected by all kinds of dynamic, ongoing, subjective processes and interactions that are difficult to define and control, and we should be prepared to adapt our conceptions according to events playing out over time.

So I stumbled on the term "relevance" to replace "power." In my original notebook entry from March 1, 2005, I defined this unified idea of motivation, the "will to relevance," as "the tendency of individuals is to persist to an (unknown) end of maximum social relevance — peer-level connections."

Google's search engine acts as a metaphor for this theory the same way that mechanical engines provided metaphors for early 20th century psychology, and, for that matter, the same way that older computing vocabularies in the mid-to-late 20th century provided metaphors for cognitive psychology.

A site's ranking in Google is affected by how many links it has to it. The more links, the more important it is supposed to be — especially when those links come from sites that also rank high by attracting a lot of links themselves. [39] So a substantial aspect of doing things online involves generating as many links to and from your site as possible, which means constantly updating the site with content that people will find useful.

It isn't altogether different from what I suspect Nietzsche meant — it essentially means optimizing self-assertion — but

---

39 Outlined by Larry Page & Sergey Brin (with their thesis advisors, Rajeev Motwani & Terry Winograd) in "The PageRank Citation Ranking: Bringing Order to the Web" (1998), at http://ilpubs.stanford.edu:8090/422/1/1999-66.pdf

"relevance" changes the connotations from *domination and control* (which have further become too saturated by mechanical metaphors), to something more organic like *connectedness and meaning.*

Mind you, connectedness and meaning may happen to manifest themselves as domination and control, but they don't have to. Connectedness may also manifest itself as altruism, and sometimes it can occur via sympathy, or curiosity, or imagination — for example, coming up with explanations for behaviour, making predictions, and rehearsing for anticipated events. The key is that everything a person does gravitates, or is conducted towards optimizing our personal sense of autonomy and self-assertion — or, to paraphrase the U.S. Army's old recruiting slogan, we're all just trying to be all we can be.

It's tough to appreciate the process because a person's state of "being" is always *becoming* something else. We're always occurring. It's difficult to capture and convey this with words and images. Various philosophers — going all the way back to Guatama Buddha, Lao Tzu, and Heraclitus — have tried explaining that "being is becoming," but these temporal explanations never seem to stick. Our spatial bias keeps drawing and anchoring us to fixed concepts. Our metaphors eventually fail; to appreciate being-as-becoming we have to practice using our own intuition and judgement.

Fortunately everybody can observe the process internally (albeit with varying degrees of accuracy); we all experience for ourselves how something difficult or off-putting one moment can become simple and desirable via a few intervening thoughts and experiences (incentives, rhetoric, rationalization — any information that changes a situation's choice architecture or fitness landscape[40]), occurring in the appropriate order, and vice versa.

---

40 "Choice architecture" is borrowed from Thaler & Sunstein's *Nudge* (2008) referring to how options are presented to, or "framed" for people. "Fitness landscape" is borrowed from biology, referring to peaks and valleys of optimal evolutionary fitness. The concept originated with Sewall Wright, "The Roles of Mutation, Inbreeding, Crossbreeding, and Selection in Evolution" (1931). Also conceived as "design space"; see *Darwin's Dangerous Idea* (1991) by Daniel Dennett.

It's important to conceive these influences not simply as pushes and pulls, but rather as walls and channels that direct, conduct, and regulate our attention and energy as we move through the temporal world, without ever stopping. We never act from an inert state, and we never face a choice of doing something versus doing nothing; we're constantly, *currently* in the process of doing or thinking something, and the choice is always among different ways to direct our attention and energy — which in a lot of cases means turning our attention inwards, to our own thoughts and stories, which we work over until an appropriate thought or circumstance compels us to direct our energy back outwards again.

What compels us to do one thing rather than something else is the relative difference in the feelings of personal efficacy we feel going into the decision. In other words, it's as if we need to be constantly reminded we exist, and the way we accomplish that is to constantly do things and make connections that produce evidence of our own existence. We make choices that optimize the probability of continuing to feel relevant and effective through to the next instant — like the way fluid and electrical currents always manage to find whichever route optimizes the *flow.*

The notion of efficacy was originally brought forward by psychologist Robert White in a classic article on what he called "effectance motivation." White focused on children and animals engaged in exploration and play. He determined from existing experiments and observations that motivation in those activities can't be understood in terms of primary drives (i.e. conceptions I would dismiss as too subject to spatial bias). He made a case for conceiving motivation as more of a process in which the subject interacts with one's environment.

If anything is being "satisfied" in this process it's our intrinsic need to feel effective and build competence. The whole notion turns on this insight: "Dealing with the environment means carrying on a continuing transaction which gradually changes one's relation to the environment. Because there is no consummatory climax, satisfaction has to be seen as lying in a considerable series of transactions, in a trend of behaviour rather than a goal that is achieved."[41]

It's an obvious precedent to Mihaly Csikszentmihalyi's now-well-known concept of flow, which refers to the process of being fully absorbed in a challenging-yet-doable activity that requires concentration and skill but seems effortless, involves goals, and generates constant feedback and growth.

Complementing both effectance and flow is the notion of "intrinsic motivation" — or more specifically "self-determination theory" described by Edward Deci and Richard Ryan. As with the ideas of White and Csikszentmihalyi, the need for competence is essential in self-determination theory. Deci and Ryan emphasized the importance of personal autonomy — i.e. to recognize that outcomes result from personal decisions, not from external interference.

Deci and Ryan also include the need for relatedness, or "organismic integration" — a process of assimilating from the environment, developing internal structures through a complex process of integration and differentiation, and accommodating oneself back out to the environment.[42]

At first glance these theories fail to address significant aspects of human psychology and behaviour — conscious planning and deliberation, for example — but I think we can overcome these apparent insufficiencies by considering that so-called "internal" experience is continuous with external experience. As Thomas Schelling put it, "the mind [is] a consuming organ."[43]

We don't have to be out interacting in the world to experience relevance (though when the opportunity is readily available, it tends to be the most effective way), because we can reminisce and reorganize our thoughts to maintain a *sense* of relevance

---

41 Robert White, "Motivation reconsidered: The concept of competence," *Psychological Review, 66* (September, 1959).

42 See Chapter 5 of Deci & Ryan's *Intrinsic Motivation and Self-Determination in Human Behavior* (1985).

43 Schelling, "The Mind As a Consuming Organ," published in *Choice and Consequence* (1984).

despite the absence of external stimuli. When external circumstances aren't satisfying our need to feel effective and relevant, we may still keep ourselves occupied by re-interpreting our memories and forming new associations in our minds.

We remind ourselves of things that happened to us in the past, we anticipate things that might happen to us in the future, and we conceive stories and reasons that place things in relation to each other — and ourselves in relation to them — and we develop a sense of ourselves as being relevant through stories and theories that we constantly maintain to assimilate and accommodate new experiences.

Both introspection and empirical research indicate that daydreaming and other cognitive experiences can feel as fulfilling as real events. Dan Ariely and Michael Norton dubbed this process "conceptual consumption," describing it as so compelling that people are even willing to sacrifice the quantity and quality of real, physical consumption for the sake of a story or an idea. They suggest several examples: buying less-favoured food for the sake of variety, being seduced by product features to buy impractical devices, not repeating special experiences for the sake of preserving memories, feeling disgust due to imagined contamination, charitable giving, and thrill-seeking.[44]

Even suicide fits into this model[45] — my interpretation of it, at least (perhaps not Ariely & Norton's notion of conceptual consumption, which I mention merely for corroboration). It's important to conceive suicide not as an opposition or denial of life, but as a kind of corrupted and pernicious attempt at self-assertion. When every idea and initiative seems to generate negative or non-corresponding feedback for a person, suicide becomes a last-ditch option to assert personal autonomy. It doesn't exactly "generate a sense of relevance through the next

---

44 Ariely & Norton, "Conceptual Consumption" in the *Annual Review of Psychology*, 60 (2009): p. 475 - 499.

45 This is *not* clinical psychology, so suicide is something I hesitate to touch on, but because it would very easily be guessed to contradict and disprove my general theory, I can't simply pass over it.

instant," but at least it doesn't generate a frustrating (and eventually intolerable) sense of *ir*relevance and inefficacy.

Applying the notion of "learned helplessness" — the sense of inefficacy or lack of control learned through negative or arbitrary feedback — is essential to understanding this process. Psychologists like Martin Seligman, Chris Peterson, and Steve Maier who've studied learned helplessness have paid special attention to how people's "explanatory styles" can affect personality. Depressed people, for example, are more likely to blame themselves for negative outcomes.[46]

More interesting to me is the process by which explanatory styles — or more precisely, the explanations themselves — might crystallize and become persistent through a person's life, and in a sense take on lives of their own, as memes, acting "selfishly" (to use Dawkins's metaphor) to replicate and perpetuate themselves, thereby affecting future ideas and actions.[47]

For example, even suicide can be profoundly influenced by ideas and stories that emerge from prior experiences and explanations. Religious ideas, cult affiliations, notions of military honour, and the prospect of after-death rewards are well known to affect people's willingness to terminate their own lives. The value that stories and ideas generate in the form of meaning, or relevance in our lives, is so important that in many cases we literally prefer to sacrifice ourselves, rather than sacrificing our ideas.

Other kinds of self-destructive behaviour have been explained in terms of "self-verification," originally by William Swann. According to self-verification theory, people actually condition their environment (i.e. choose relationships and cue the people they interact with) in a way that reinforces self-concepts they already have — even if they're negative — in order to maximize

---

46 Peterson, Maier, and Seligman, *Learned Helplessness* (1993).

47 Daniel Dennett provides a good introduction to the notion of memes, aka "cultural symbionts" in *Freedom Evolves* (2003): Chapter 6, "The Evolution of Open Minds."

a sense of predictability and control (essentially the same principle that underlying the notion of learned helplessness). [48]

My feeling is self-verification theory can be generalized simply as "verification theory." People seem to gravitate into circumstances that are most likely to appear to corroborate their ideas about the world in general (and specific objects and people in the world), not just ideas about themselves — though, as I mentioned earlier, one's self is the centre of one's experience, and since everything experienced and conceived is experienced and conceived *by the person*, ideas about *every*thing are infused (or shaded) with notions of *personal relevance* and at least indirectly contribute to one's sense of self.

Just as ideas and stories can have ill effects on our subjective well-being, they're also the means by which we bring ourselves up, make ourselves happier and more competent, and ultimately contribute to a better society. Just as we can use explanatory styles to learn helplessness, we can use them to learn optimism. Just as we can condition our circumstances to reinforce negative concepts, we can condition the world to reinforce positive concepts.

Dan McAdams's research on "life stories" covers some of these notions together. [49] Specifically he has developed the notion of "redemptive" life stories, which reinforce positive notions of overcoming hardships, gratitude, good work, giving back and investing not just for one's own future (and not just financially) but for the benefit of later generations and purposes greater than themselves. [50]

An especially vivid example of this (albeit perhaps a fictional one) is found in Plato's *Crito*, in which Socrates argues it is better for him to be executed than to flee from Athens. Because

---

48 William Swann et al., "The Allure of Negative Feedback: Self-Verification Strivings Among Depressed Persons," in the *Journal of Abnormal Psychology*, Vol. 101, No. 2 (May 1992): p. 293 - 306.

49 Covered by Dan McAdams, "Personal Narratives and the Life Story" in *Handbook of Personality: Theory and Research,* ed. Robins & Pervin (2008): p. 241 - 261.

50 "The Redemptive Self: Generativity and the Stories Americans Live By," *Research in Human Development* (2006): p. 81 - 100.

he had invested so much of his life in the laws and culture of the city, if he fled he be severing that connection — not just to Athens, but to the notions of reason and justice for which it stands, and which he spent his life fighting and arguing for. In other words, he sacrificed himself to save his life story — a story explicitly connected to future generations, and which profoundly influenced Western civilization through the personal narratives of its greatest thinkers, St. Augustine to Nietzsche.

Again, the key is to understand that people aren't the basic unit of social and psychological development; rather, it's more effective to appreciate that it's ideas themselves (i.e. memes) defining the process. The question of altruism, for example, becomes easier to account for by saying that people make sacrifices for the sake of *redemptive narratives* (i.e. stories that *espouse* sacrifices for the sake of other individuals and society as a whole) or *conceptual consumption*, rather than trying to identify individuals as inherently altruistic (or non-altruistic) and then hoping to contrive sophisticated schemes for explaining exceptional behaviour.

There's a bit of a hitch here: I've been leaving a lot of ambiguity between "ideas" and "stories." My definitions for both are very broad: "ideas" are any distinguishable unit of cognitive stuff, stories are ideas or combinations of ideas of events (or just one event) playing out over time. A story by my definition could be as simple as a statement of cause and effect. By that definition, "theories" are also stories.

Now there's another difficulty: conceptualizing stories as memes. Some stories can be very complex and dynamic (especially life stories). Different people often come away from the same event with different stories, and we're often still within stories while we're still in the process of narrating them — so the story can change as we tell it, and sometimes it's act of telling a story that changes it.

It's tough to imagine such amorphous stories as being analogous to gene-like replicators; there is too much adaptation occurring *within* the narrative process itself. But here we can mine digital media for useful metaphors. We can observe how snippets of text (or pictures or sounds or both) can be copied and recombined and propagated across the Web. We can see how comments become reputations, conversations become communities, tweets become blog posts — and perhaps eventually books (which is exactly how a lot of ideas found their way into *this* book and the story I tell about it; the book is its own metaphor).

We can learn to intuit the processes through which memes proliferate and associate with each other to affect decisions, beginning by determining the choices present in circumstances, then the way in which a person's attention will be drawn to each of them, the way in which they will be conceived, etc. For example, joining a Facebook group might change the ads you'll see. Using a specific word on Twitter could lead to a few new followers, which could lead to new friends, which changes the stream of information you see flowing around you, which changes the kinds of comments you're likely to make in the future, which will change how you appear in searches, and so on. Every click, link, and like we make online changes the system somehow, which reflects back to us.

Our physical, social, and conceptual actions have always occurred like that. Both the content and the manner of our communications affects what people think and feel about us, consequently influencing how they approach us (if at all) and what sort of opportunities they're willing to present.

On one level, relevance on the Web isn't merely a metaphor for motivation; it's an actual demonstration. The Web is a laboratory where we can watch the will to relevance play out, both in real time and cumulatively, as people click and share links, find and be found, develop relationships, and cultivate communities.

Online relevance means more than just maximizing subscribers and links, it's also about optimizing the appropriateness, context, integrity, vitality, richness, and reciprocity of those connections: it's about how *effective and alive* our relations are. The value of the *subjective relevance* of Kevin Kelly's proverbial

"1000 true fans"[51] and a dozen genuine friends may be far greater than the value of the *objective relevance* of 1,000,000 Twitter followers or 5000 Facebook "friends."

There has been some discussion about the value of follows on Twitter who come by way of a list that automatically suggests popular users to new registrants. People popular enough to get on the list saw their follower statistics skyrocket, but at least one prominent blogger made a case that while the numbers are high, the followers represented by them are not actually engaging.[52]

Briefly turning the discussion back to political philosophy, consider authoritarian dictators who may have a lot of objective relevance in the number of people under their thumb, but their subjective relevance may be fairly low. They don't necessarily interact meaningfully — not just despite being able to dictate to anyone, but because of that, there can be a lack of genuine engagement and reciprocity. And in a way, the mass population they rule over relates to them as merely one single connection.

Putting principles aside, it's interesting to consider authoritarian psychology through the lens of effectance motivation and the will to relevance. Remember that what's needed is a constant stream of feedback. If you control everything, if your connections aren't free to generate connections on your behalf or develop more relevance autonomously (which would increase the relevance they feed back to you), then eventually you find yourself on a treadmill of diminishing returns, having to do more and more — likely tending to be increasingly despotic — to maintain the same sense of relevance.

Likewise for all the people living under an authoritarian regime, or even working in a large organization, or just temporarily part of an audience assembled around a common, central or frontal focal point (e.g. attending a movie, a concert, or a lecture): there are connections, but they don't distinguish

---

51 "1000 True Fans," by Kevin Kelly at kk.org/thetechnium (March 4, 2008).
52 "Nobody Has a Million Twitter Followers" by Anil Dash at dashes.com (Jan. 5, 2010).

any individual from any other so they don't generate a very deep or enduring sense of relevance.

Well managed Facebook and Twitter accounts generate continuous streams of experience that are appropriate, vital, rich, and reciprocal — *relevant*. But Facebook can still fall way short — especially if it isn't managed properly. It often favours the immediate and superficial — games like Farmville and Mafia Wars — becoming another hedonic treadmill.

As tools and practices for managing these applications develop, those criticisms are less true now than they were even a year or two ago. Facebook has improved its filtering so people only have to see what's most interesting and useful — away from games, more towards conversations (or at least comments). This demonstrates my point even further: we need connections that are meaningful, substantial, and dynamic. We may often be seduced by passing fancies and immediate gratifications, but eventually we need relationships and communities that (while they're impossible to control, and often generate uncertainty) eventually develop a kind of life of their own, extending beyond our own personal will, generating more value than what we put it, working on the principle of investment.

Think about the kind of happiness that comes from love and belonging. Marriage and family relationships generate a lot of personal relevance — relevance that lives and grows with us (rather than more temporary kinds of push-button relevance, which incur constant costs of attention that deliver diminishing returns). When we identify with people so closely there is a lot of high quality relevance experienced vicariously, or in sympathy with them — experiencing their successes (and failures) and growth as part of your own success and growth.

Your kids will grow up to have their kids, proliferating on your behalf the connections and human relevance you have in the world. Think of a grandparent watching a grandchild playing. Think of how much emotional capital and subjective relevance is infused in that experience. While the child is inclined to explore and do all sorts of mischievous, arbitrary things to experience a sense of efficacy, the grandparent experiences the same scene as affirmation. In a sense, the child *is* their effect and a constant source of feedback — a reminder that they're alive and have a relevant place in the world.

Religious beliefs and other sorts of cultural values and principles are perhaps more interesting. It may be suggested that religious people are happy because they are integrated into a support community, or they tend to live less stressful lives; but consider the sense of relevance experienced by true believers: every event is potentially another reminder and apparent *verification* of their belief, and a justification of their existence.

Seeing our stories and ideas validated by events in the real world is a satisfying experience. Sometimes a little creative interpretation is required to make our beliefs accord with reality (and vice versa), but that creative aspect is largely what makes it so gratifying. It's like a conversation. It's about developing a kind of rapport with the universe. Just as a proud grandparent experiences joy in identifying with their grandchildren, a true believer experiences joy in every turn of fate, confident that their God is behind it all.

We're learning that people aren't motivated just by money and trophies but by the process itself. People want *meaning* — i.e. a sense of touching the means to something greater than one's self — and a sense of relevance that comes not *only* from static trophies and particular accomplishments (though those are still essential) but from life itself as it occurs.

If you conceive yourself as a stable unit — something like a billiard ball or a car — rolling, bouncing, and "driving" towards goals across a landscape, you're not leaving much room for personal growth. We're more complex, ambiguous, and dynamic than our conventional assumptions about our selves. We're more like snowballs, changing and being changed by the landscape as we move through it. But even that fails to represent life's fluid and emergent character.

This process also helps us understand learning more effectively. Consider Csikszentmihalyi's notion of flow again, as it "fosters the *expansion* of an individual's set of enjoyed pursuits," rather than simply satisfying drives.[53] In other words, because we're

53 "The Construction of Meaning Through Vital Engagement" by Nakamura

constantly learning and adapting through the process, it's difficult to predict from one moment to the next precisely how compelling or doable an experience will be, because different experiences affect a person's preparedness for other experiences.

When we develop new skills and work up to new challenges, we're not just experiencing relevance, we're also making it easier to find and manage relevance in the future. Learning means *investing in relevance* — which means investing in long-term happiness. It makes us more effective, which doesn't just mean we increase productivity and reduce anxiety; effectiveness and relevance are essentially ends in themselves.

& Csikszentmihalyi in *Flourishing*, Haidt, ed. (2003 [my emphasis]. *The Evolving Self* (1993) is the book to read on flow as it relates to complexity science.

8 Creating an Open Society

The way our long-term explanations, beliefs, and intentions take shape is largely determined by which ideas consistently manage to "fit" circumstances and sustain themselves by staying relevant, making new connections, and generating more uses.

It's as if our ideas are literally "attracted" to the kinds of causal roles they're qualified for. Our ideas seem to constantly move into opportunities to connect in more relevant ways, just as we do. When we observe things happening in the world, specific ideas step forward to nominate themselves for attribution, and we act or express ourselves (or continue to think) in some way shaped by the idea.

Frequently, thoughts and actions are affected by chance variations. Remember the provision that sometimes people do things because they must be doing *some*thing, if only because everything has temporal qualities. This is often how discoveries and creative works come to be made. In fact, the definitions of discovery and creation essentially require that they are unexpected.

This analogy between creativity and the evolutionary process has been studied and made explicit by psychologists for well over a century. Research indicates that creatively successful people owe their success primarily to a willingness to try more things than most people do. By virtue of generating more ideas and trying more combinations — and producing many failures in the process — they eventually produce more successes as well.[54]

Shortly after the publication of Darwin's *Origins of Species*, the notion of natural selection was almost immediately taken up by philosophers like Herbert Spencer to enlighten or explain cognitive processes. William James did the same; in fact he

---

54 Dean Keith Simonton, *Origins of Genius* (1999).

pointed out that Spencer's theory wasn't Darwinian enough. Historian Robert J. Richards summarizes James's correction of Spencer, telling us James believed that "the novel ideas produced by men of genius — and ourselves on occasion — were not due to direct adaptations," but rather "sprang up in the mind as spontaneous mental variations..." [55]

Of course, it isn't enough just to generate wild and random ideas. Creative geniuses spend years (usually about ten) gaining enough "domain-relevant knowledge and skills," to be able to recognize and capitalize on their novel ideas. As Louis Pasteur famously said, "chance favours the prepared mind."

In that time, creative people develop what Howard Gruber called a "network of enterprise" — not merely a handful of discreet projects, but a dynamic system of related interests and activities. Networks of enterprise enable creators to adapt and keep working when unexpected barriers and opportunities emerge, as "an insight in one project may reawaken a dormant enterprise. A new skill mastered in the interests of one enterprise may suddenly become relevant elsewhere in the tangle." [56]

It's no coincidence that the Web is essentially a large-scale model of the same kinds of processes. Tim Berners-Lee's idea for the World Wide Web was deliberately modeled after the human mind's ability to generate new, meaningful associations.. [57]

On a practical level he wanted to design a better system for finding relevant expertise within a large, complex institution. On a more ambitious level he was re-imagining how people collaborate and create.

Creativity occurs in different ways in different realms — often in different silos. We're all familiar with these barriers within and between organizations, but on an even deeper level there

---

55 Richards, *Darwin and the Emergence of Evolutionary Theories of Mind and Behavior* (1989): pg. 427.

56 Howard Gruber, "An Evolving Systems Approach to Creative Work" in *Creative People at Work,* edited by Wallace & Gruber (1992): p. 20.

57 Tim Berners-Lee, *Weaving the Web* (1999).

are certain assumptions and conventions preventing us from seeing the connections between art, science, commerce, civics, etc.

My sense is that even these general categories will have to be re-conceived. The future I imagine now is one in which all of these aspects of our society have become closely integrated, almost unified in some aspects, while being re-differentiated across different axes. It isn't just a few ideas here and there that are being re-organized; our most basic assumptions about what it means to be an artist, researcher, entrepreneur, and activist are variously converging and diverging into new categories.

Keep in mind that the ongoing process of conceiving and investigating new possibilities is purposeful in itself. And remember that the key to creativity is freedom and availability to form new associations. This imaginative, speculative approach will generate a lot of mistakes — but without the mistakes we won't generate any creative insights or opportunities.

Also remember that none of us have to do any of this brainstorming ourselves (though I happen to enjoy it). Creativity is increasingly a social process, facilitated by markets and organizations, in which innovations aren't generated by individual geniuses but by organizations and networks working together.

Big corporations can be slow and stodgy, but in general, commercial enterprise has an astonishing ability to adapt and grow.

Look at Silicon Valley; it's a kind of "entangled bank" of entrepreneurial activity, with researchers, founders, employees, and investors constantly forming new, often spontaneous associations complementing each other.

Every year, thousands of entrepreneurial startups around the world — think of them as "chance variations" — are born, becoming either "selected" to thrive or reabsorbed back into the chaos from which new associations may emerge. A lot of startups fail, but the ones that succeed keep investors in business, circulating capital back to the entrepreneurs.

As with any kind of creativity, it's impossible to know how well any particular idea will work out until it's tried. The more ideas you try, the more likely you are to have one that succeeds. In this way, success doesn't occur despite failure, it occurs because of it — as long as you're actually learning, cultivating some kind of mastery in the process, and continually re-investing towards the future, and not failing to the point of catastrophe.

On a smaller level some of the most successful companies recreate this evolutionary process on a smaller scale within themselves, encouraging employees to experiment, play, and try new ideas knowing that eventually a few will turn out successfully. Google famously keeps services in beta for years after "launching early and launching often" [58] so they can get information on how to improve as quickly as possible.

Paradoxically, it's this redundancy and unpredictable dynamism that makes systems sustainable over the long term. It's the constant experimentation, failure, and iteration that keeps things evolving. If the system became too homogeneous and stable it would become inbred and vulnerable. [59]

The challenge for people who genuinely want to understand these processes is to appreciate that successful and apparently stable organizations, practices, and ideas, rather than having some kind of inherent merit that makes them exceptions to the rule of failure, are essentially just experiments that were fortunate to work for their time and place — experiments that haven't failed *yet*.

Look at the history of any great company and notice how much their success relied on serendipity: a chance introduction that

---

58 Quoting Marissa Mayer, Google's V.P of Search Product and User Experience on Charlie Rose's TV show (March 5, 2009). She was paraphrasing "release early, release often," a notion that developed with the open source Linux project, as described by Eric Raymond in *The Cathedral and the Bazaar* (2000): available online at http://www.catb.org/~esr/writings/homesteading/cathedral-bazaar/ar01s04.html

59 See Nassim Taleb's *Black Swan* (2007) and Clayton Christensen's *Innovator's Dilemma* (1997) on unexpected events and disruptive technology respectively.

forms a partnership, a spontaneous insight leading to innovation, a couple of key hires that created unique team chemistry, a few gut decisions that luckily turned out well — aided by bad decisions by key competitors, etc.

That isn't to diminish the importance of hard work and persistence. The other side of the coin is that when people believe they can't fail, they're less likely to. Appreciating our creative and entrepreneurial enterprises as experiments means accepting on one hand that most people who try something genuinely creative, believing they can't fail, end up failing, but on the other hand, virtually nobody who anticipates failure ends up succeeding.

But too often, desire for success turns into a willingness to cut corners, embellish results, manipulate appearances, and game the system. Those behaviours undermine the process.

The whole process relies on failure. People have to be willing to accept failure and admit to mistakes, or the process won't work. If we artificially hide information to deny failures — whether it's done in the name of optimism or is simply a manifestation of greediness — then the process becomes toxic and corroded, errors fester unnoticed, and catastrophe-making chain reactions are set in motion.

As long as we live in a world in which there are barriers and profound disincentives to saying, "sorry, I don't understand," or "I screwed up," we'll keep losing our grip on our economic and social challenges.

This brings me back to the refrain I've used throughout this book: the process of creation and discovery *is itself* the answer. When it's ok to love learning for its own sake — rather than assuming education is merely something that goes on a résumé — then we don't have to worry about how to motivate people to solve unexpected problems, because solving unexpected problems is intrinsically rewarding.

But to be able to solve emerging problems and create new opportunities effectively, we need access to all of the pertinent information. The process doesn't work if a few organizations artificially maintain their own relevance and control by erecting barriers and withholding information.

My ideal is summed up simply by Karl Popper's description of an open society as a society that "sets free the critical powers of man."[60] Popper's ideas and criticisms were an attempt to infuse the whole public sphere with the spirit of science — not as something that presumes to find out what the truth will always be (which would be an excuse from critical responsibilities — which is perhaps precisely why that attitude is so compelling to some) but rather as a process of constantly testing and refining our assumptions.

More importantly, science means *allowing others* to test and refine our assumptions as well. This is where my belief in open government comes from: not some vague, principled need to let everyone express their opinion, but rather a process of submitting decisions to scrutiny from more perspectives, to reveal where subjective biases and false assumptions might be affecting the process, to ensure the whole system doesn't become vulnerable to the intrinsic fallibilities and weaknesses of a few individuals.

Popper distinguished that to be scientific about social issues does not mean deriving ideas from a supposedly solid foundation of scientific evidence, but rather appreciating all of our predictions and plans (and the assumptions they're based on) as hypotheses to be falsified or provisionally corroborated by objective results.

This notion — the importance of appreciating fallibility — was outlined earlier by Charles Sanders Peirce,[61] and is a integral to pragmatist philosophy, which will be taken up in the next chapter. This attitude is an essential element of my thinking, prediction-making, and planning. For example, if I turn out to be wrong about what I've written about the future of things

---

60 Karl Popper, *The Open Society and Its Enemies* (1962, Princeton 1971): V. 1, p. 1.

61 See "The Fixation of Belief" (1877), *Collected Papers*: V. 8; p. 223 - 247. Also "The First Rule of Logic" (1898) in the same volume: see especially p. 408 - 410.

(e.g. newspapers, government, education), I can trace my thinking back to these ideas so I can find and correct my mistakes. It's a kind of "conceptual accounting."

More importantly, *you* can trace my thinking back to get a better sense of where I'm coming from. And if you've kept an account of your thinking, I can follow that back too. If we have a disagreement we can compare notes and look for the inconsistencies, then try to "inter-subjectively" identify the best ideas. Subsequently, we shouldn't come away from that conversation with the feeling that one person won and the other lost, we can come away feeling that we're both engaged in an ongoing process of *learning*.

It's important to appreciate that when approaching challenges in this manner, decisions are never final. Whenever we "solve" a problem, or make any kind of decision, we shouldn't just say, "There's that problem solved" and forget about it. I try to treat every idea as a prototype or experiment that needs to be followed-up on and assessed. We need to actively watch the results to see how the solution is performing — and not be surprised or defensive when it performs poorly — and make adjustments accordingly.

Again, it comes down to the love of learning. If you genuinely want to learn, then this approach will come naturally (with some supplemental discipline). If you don't genuinely want to learn, you'll be tempted to use persuasion and positive thinking to deflect people's attention (including your own) away from mistakes and weaknesses.

This is not just idealism on my part. In just the past few years we've seen a real, pronounced opening-up of the decision-making processes in business and government. Companies aren't just soliciting feedback from customers; by using the Internet they're able to find conversations where and when they occur, in real time, and because these digital comments are already documented and measurable, they immediately generate usable analytics that can affect a company's decisions with relatively little interpretation required.

Feedback is even richer and more useful when the product or service itself is digitized and networked. Companies can get an immediate sense of what users like and don't like. So much more development is now done after an application is released.

Twitter is an especially prominent example. After launching as a minimalist service, users began to develop specialized practices and semantic conventions (for example, using @ to address messages to specific individuals and # to tag messages with topical or event-specific keywords) which were later coded directly into the service. Other developers have also been free to make complementary applications for updating, reading, and analysing Twitter — to such a degree that many people rarely even visit the website itself.

The company and its founders couldn't have possibly thought of all of these features and functions. Even if they could, they still wouldn't have had enough resources to develop them — certainly not when you consider how much time and energy went into developing all of the unsuccessful applications, without which it might not have been possible to recognize the few truly useful ones.

Again we come back to the evolutionary characteristics of these social and technological "ecosystems." There is virtually no risk for individual users to play around with using @ and # in their tweets, whereas if Twitter had assumed too much certainty about how people would eventually use the service, they might have created barriers to those developments and the service might have been a failure as a whole.

If that had been the case, the loss would not just have been Twitter itself; we would have lost the opportunity for all of the innovative and interesting uses it generated — i.e. the way it has opened up media and marketing backchannels where information is shared and these kinds of ideas are discussed. This is ultimately what it's all about. Applications are just tools; the truly profound innovations are going to be social and institutional ways to facilitate greater autonomy and relevance — a phase that's only just beginning.

Just as these generative networks are open to relatively low risk experiments, they're also open to more objective observation and evaluation. And the resulting criticisms and conversations themselves are open to criticism. In turn, that process affects individual reputations — and these are open to objective criticism as well: we can look at people's past statements, we can look at exactly who supports them, etc, and we assess how they fit with the rest of our connections.

Here once again, our experience with the Web is our way to understand even greater possibilities. Because we can observe how software platforms evolve and develop, we can get a better sense of how this process can be used to improve our organizations and institutions themselves — all the way up to the notion of what Tim O'Reilly calls "government as a platform."[62]

It's time to seriously re-conceive what democracy can be. Elections and other democratic traditions developed to fi t social circumstances that have since evolved. Not only do we have better tools for many tasks, we have *different* tasks. Our challenges are also more complex — requiring expertise so specialized it's tough even to *find* the appropriate expert.

By conceiving government as a kind of ongoing, open source project, people with the appropriate skills and knowledge for specific needs are able to self-select and contribute more effectively — whether by joining an actual project, or independently developing an application that taps into open data. In such a system, innovative solutions and opportunities are more likely to be discovered. Because of the relatively low risks on experimentation, it occurs within a larger, diverse ecosystem of collaborators and critics who constantly fi lter and absorb failure while naturally propagating the most effective practices and ideas.

Understanding open government requires a signifi cant shift in mindset, starting with the notion that government's fi rst responsibility is to improve itself — not in an idealistic, "rebuild it from the ground-up" sort of way, but simply in a way that approaches every project as a learning experience,

---

62 "Government As a Platform" in *Open Government,* edited by Lathrop & Ruma (2010): p. 11 - 39.

every policy as a hypothesis that we expect to re-evaluate as we move forward, which improves our understanding and helps us answer the next set of questions.

To make that turn, we need to think and frame things in terms of collaboration rather than deliberation. [63] That means *making* things, prototyping and iterating, seeing what works and using real observations to ground ongoing decisions. [64] This will require a considerable shift in how we think about "leadership," for example. Leaders need to think like builders rather than merely bosses[65] — learning through the decision-making process as a kind of design process.[66]

We still need criticism and dialog, but dialog needs to refer to what we're actually *doing* — things we're trying, experiments that will generate objective, observable results — rather than merely arguing and trying to persuade each other with increasingly costly rhetoric.

Obviously on most issues such an approach isn't feasible — and hardly even conceivable — yet. But there are plenty of challenges we *can* start addressing this way, specifically improvements to our information and communications infrastructures. By approaching those challenges with much larger possibilities in mind, our experience through them will provide the verification or falsification we need to outline a larger strategy — if such a strategy is feasible at all. We can't know for sure until we experiment.

Above all, it requires a growth mindset. [67] We need to accept that everything is a work in progress, nothing is perfect, and this fact is not something to lament; it's something to celebrate.

---

63 See Beth Simone Noveck, *Wiki Government* (2009) or "The Single Point of Failure" in *Open Government* (2010): p. 60.

64 See Tim Brown's *Change By Design* (2009) for an elaboration on how this iterative "design thinking" process works.

65 Umair Haque, "The Builders' Manifesto" at HBR Blogs (December 18, 2009): http://blogs.hbr.org/haque/2009/12/the_builders_manifesto.html

66 IDEO's Colin Raney & Ryan Jacoby, "Decisions by Design: Stop Deciding, Start Designing," in *Rotman Magazine* (Winter 2010).

67 Carol Dweck, *Mindset: The New Psychology of Success* (2007).

What's life for if not to aspire and work towards something better? This is what "openness" means in the fullest sense; not just transparent, but open-ended — *open to the future,* and generative[68] like the process of evolution itself.

An open society needs to engage people's interests, competencies, and passions. Sustainable systems of participation have to provide opportunities for fl ow and conceptual consumption, to receive feedback, to socialize, to recognize we actually have an effect on the world — specifically, to recognize our effects as *uniquely and autonomously* our own, which fit with our personal identities and stories, not effects that are indistinguishable and generic — to place ourselves in relation to others, to learn, and to know that our life ultimately means something bigger and more enduring than what we're given.

As I've argued throughout this book, such a process isn't merely a means to building a better society, such a process *is itself* the better society we want. Collaborative, dynamic, learning-oriented processes are intrinsically gratifying and generative. A society in which such processes fl ourish — and enable each of us to, in our own distinctive, and relevant ways — is *already* a better society.

---

68 On "generative technology" and enterprise, the book to read is Jonathan Zittrain's *Future of the Internet--And How to Stop It* (2008).

9 A Sense of the Future

In the midst of so much talk about the end of print and quality in journalism, Lewis Lapham, defiantly launched an expensive quarterly full of big ideas, curated largely from the past. The inaugural issue began with an essay about history: "Construed as a means instead of an end, history is the weapon with which we defend the future against the past."[69]

It may seem like a contradiction; it might seem that history has more to do with preserving the past while delaying or avoiding the future. Admittedly, this is often true: some people abuse history as an excuse to turn away from the present and the future. One of Nietzsche's earliest works was an argument that history is often abused as a way to avoid addressing the present.

So what about the *use* of history? Jacques Barzun answered this question with characteristic simplicity and directness: "The use of history is for the person." Seems obvious enough, but it's apparently easy to forget, perhaps especially in the education system.

Studying history is about educating oneself for the present and future, not just preserving or restoring the past. Barzun wrote that history provides something that neither science nor art can: an intuitive sense for "continuity in chaos... attainment in the heart of disorder... purpose." Science denies this sense, while "art only invents it."[70]

You could argue that science does provide a sense of purpose, and that art provides it in a really genuine way as well, but consider that such ways are essentially historical. Science and art have histories (and biographies) like every other human endeavour; it is mainly through history and biography — or

---

69 "The Gulf of Time" in *Lapham's Quarterly* (Winter 2008).
70 *Clio and the Doctors* (1974): p. 124.

simply, through stories — that they converge and become relevant in our lives.

It might be difficult to recognize the importance of history in this regard because it's so deeply habituated in us; we tend to take it for granted, thinking of it as plain old common sense, which demands no further elaboration.

If I read it correctly, Barzun's argument is that history is common sense which has been educated and refined through conscientious research and composition; history is common sense becoming a more comprehensive "logic of events."

History is like science in that it involves discipline and produces falsifiable results; we can objectively evaluate the merits of historians and their works by checking their accordance with trustworthy facts and practices. But history is not as severely limited by methods and formulas as science. History relies a lot more on the historian's sensibilities and judgement in selecting and ordering facts.

We might say that all scientific and artistic achievements begin and end as history. All scientists and artists begin with some kind of common (or historical) sense — an "untaught knowledge of how the world goes"; when this sense is violated — by some fact or event that defies it — scientists and artists are moved to make an account of it. If the account is successful, then it will occupy a place in the history of human achievement; even after it is surpassed by later successes, even after it is proved false or has been replaced by other styles, it is still potentially useful as history.

This is perhaps most apparent in biographies of scientists and artists; history humanizes what may otherwise be inaccessible or uninteresting. History reassures us that Newton and Shakespeare didn't come from some superhuman realm, bringing fully formed talents and infallible ideas without context; it reminds us that the great natural philosopher struggled through mistakes and self-doubt like anyone else might, and even the great poet owed as much to circumstances and history as he owed to intrinsic genius.

History helps us to associate and discern. In his great essay on the subject, Emerson described history as a record of the "works of universal mind" — a continuous intellectual enterprise — access to which is available to anyone who would "read history actively and not passively; to esteem his own life in the text":

"What Plato has thought, he may think; what a saint has felt, he may feel; what at any time has befallen any man, he can understand. ...

"So all that is said of the wise man by Stoic or Oriental or modern essayist, describes to each reader his own idea, describes his unattained but attainable self. "

The "unattained but attainable self" is the organ that both uses and makes history — or uses history to make history — to live more creatively and effectively.

People don't merely live, we tend to live *for* something, or *towards* something — something we feel, think, and believe is the purpose of life, or simply some ideal sense of self we're inclined to aspire to by way of personal narratives. People want to be remembered as good-hearted, hard-working, intelligent, popular, accomplished, redemptive, loved.[71]

Many people are content to live and work towards objects that already exist — acquiring prize possessions and accomplishments. As I discussed in "Common Aspirations," I worry that our society has become too obsessed with following the crowd in pursuit of rivalrous goals that keep us on separate treadmills.

Some of us are compelled towards objects that don't exist yet — opportunities to discover or create something new. This is the essence of the "radically creative" personality and the attitude I hope to promote. Unlike people who chase goals that are already highly recognized, radically creative people "buy low

---

71 Unfortunately, as discussed in "Will to Relevance," many people live through negative stories of helplessness and victimization.

and sell high,"[72] staying alert to opportunities that haven't been noticed.

Creative people are drawn to fill perceived gaps in fields of research, markets, communities, or realms of aesthetic experience. These "gaps" might be revealed by conflicting sets of practices, such as the tension between old and new media, or gaps might occur as scientific anomalies and inconsistencies such as the theoretical differences between quantum mechanics and Einstein's general relativity.

The key is that radically creative people ultimately define their own opportunities, articulating what was once ambiguous rather than accepting given frameworks, motivated by what Michael Polanyi described as "heuristic passion" demonstrated by scientists as they pursue what are essentially hunches. [73] He suggested that scientific discoveries as beginning with "solitary intimations of a problem, of bits and pieces here and there which seem to offer clues to something hidden. They look like fragments of a yet unknown coherent whole... its content is undefinable, indeterminate, strictly personal."[74]

That's how scientists, artists, and entrepreneurs work. Creative opportunities don't stand out like trophies or rise like mountains to be conquered (these are more often *results* of creativity). Rather, creative opportunities begin as *openings* — like doorways, or like the mouth of Plato's allegorical cave, opening out to an unknown world — or a water well that needs to be dug, or an unsightly city block that can be turned into a park or community garden, or an algorithm for organizing information that scales with the Web, or a new platform for keeping people connected and up-to-date with each other's activities and interests.

A lot of creative projects are disruptive — taking relevance away from older means of conceptual consumption, undermining established social and conceptual frameworks.

---

72 "Investment theory of creativity" is borrowed from Sternberg & Lubart, *Defying the Crowd: Cultivating Creativity in a Culture of Conformity* (1995).

73 See *Personal Knowledge* (1958) p. 142 - 145.

74 *The Tacit Dimension* (1966): p. 75 - 76. Also in *Meaning* (1977): p. 193.

This is inevitable. Economist Joseph Schumpeter called it "creative destruction," an essentially evolutionary process conducted "not merely due to the fact that economic life goes on in a social and natural environment which changes," but more importantly via the constant regeneration of "new consumers, goods, the new methods of production or transportation, the new markets, the new forms of industrial organization that capitalist enterprise creates." [75]

The most resilient elements of humanity aren't things held rigid for their own sake, but things that are dynamic and adaptive. Even the most apparently permanent human creations — conceptual and architectural structures — decay over time, and become derelict if unused for too long. In other words, they exist for the sake of what we can *make* of them, not for their own sake. Though we might preserve them for the purpose of nostalgia or narrative historical reference, eventually everything is succeeded via generative cycles, as the young replace the old.

It's essential to appreciate that this process is generated from the bottom up, or through a flux of personal choices. You don't have to be an Enronian, "greed is good" capitalist to recognize that people's individual needs and desires change over time — because as long as time exists, things will continue changing — and *we'll* continue changing. As we each seek new experiences, more information, improved health and well-being, stronger relationships, more sustainable communities, and a more vivid sense of autonomous selfhood, we're constantly rewiring the webs of social and conceptual relevance through which people find creative opportunities.

Even people without any especially creative aspirations feed the process. Everyone is engaged in telling a story, cultivating relevance, and "placing one's self in relation to others" by means of conceptual consumption, even if only by using and endorsing (essentially voting for) the ideas, practices, and goals that others have made. Through this process, dissipative social structures emerge — not as fixed foundations, but rather as

---

75 *Capitalism, Socialism, and Democracy* (1942): p. 82.

dynamic systems that conduct and regulate life's temporal aspect, as characterized by our aspirations and our need for a sense of personal efficacy. Everything begins and ends with our personal choices and the sense of self we generate through stories incorporating the people, objects, and ideas around us.

In this way, Emerson's "unattained but attainable self" is like Polanyi's "unknown coherent whole." The future is a kind of problem (or opportunity) to be resolved and accounted for. It doesn't have to be a ground-breaking scientific problem; sometimes we're simply trying to define who we are — i.e. you might just care about what the future will be *for you*. Even people who "leave it to fate" by saying "whatever happens, happens," aren't avoiding the problem; they merely resolve it in an uncreative way, by filling the gap with a conceptual dud.

In a way, such people actually aspire to be ineffective and ungenerative. They generate a passive ideal from their intuitive sense of life as having no purpose — or at least not enough purpose to be willingly and responsibly engaged — and this becomes their main assumption about life: their horizon of attainability stops at perceived helplessness.

But a more active and conscientious exposure to history, which goes beyond immediate experience and common sense, introduces many facts that contradict and challenge the notion of helplessness. History provides examples of great accomplishments and accounts of how they occurred, which invariably involve some combination of active attention and personal will.

These facts thus poke holes in idealizations of helplessness, creating new problems to be resolved, which hopefully lead to a more vivid sense of purpose: How can you say that whatever happens, happens, when history demonstrates that what happens largely depends what people *do*?

So history can be used to demonstrate that life means the purposeful *act* of living, not merely something given to passive recipients. As Barzun said, history's use is to provide an intuitive sense of purpose, or "attainment in the heart of disorder."

José Ortega y Gasset, a philosopher who was obsessed with history, calls this notion of personal becoming a "vital project." Unlike something inert like a stone, which "is given its existence," a person "has to be himself in spite of unfavourable circumstances; that means he has to make his own existence at every single moment."[76] In other words, each person is "something which is not yet but aspires to be."

Steven Pinker has used these statements by Ortega as an example of the "blank slate" argument,[77] which he opposes — and which I think Ortega would oppose too. Ortega was writing metaphorically; he was exaggerating to make an ambitiously metaphysical point about the creative aspect of human nature, which distinguishes us from the rest of nature.

Ortega wasn't afraid to amplify some claims for literary effect. As with Nietzsche, it is fairly easy to find a few quotes and phrases in his work to give colour to all kinds of radical positions, without bothering to read more deeply for his underlying message or purpose.

Now it strikes me that this itself is a demonstration of our relationship with the world, and thus our sense of the future. You can't get a fair account of Ortega's purpose from the few phrases that you might receive from people like me and Steven Pinker, just as you won't get a fair account of life's purpose from the few impressions you might happen to passively receive. We must continually work it out for ourselves.

Life presents a lot of information — far more than we could ever actually recognize and address — from which we select only what interests us, or what concerns us, or what threatens our existing knowledge. From these limited selections we compose our stories and conceptual accounts.

The most accurate scientific accounts tend to be generated from the largest and most diverse samples. A survey that carefully selects 100,000 people from a representative cross-section of society will be far more useful than a survey of subscribers to a

---

76 José Ortega y Gasset, *History as a System* (1941/1961): p. 111.
77 Steven Pinker, *The Blank Slate* (2002): p. 24.

special-interest magazine, or an arbitrary survey of people who happen to be walking through the local mall on a weekday.

As in science, an effort must be made to generate fair and diverse samples for our historical or common sense accounts of life. In some cases this calls for restraint, cutting off impressions that might be too biassed or unrepresentative; in other cases it means going out in search of new impressions to help fill in gaps — and studying history is one of the most effective ways to find more facts and impressions. Above all it involves active attention and personal will; care and conviction; discretion and aspiration; responsibility, respect, resourcefulness, and resolve.

The analogy with survey samples isn't quite accurate. Historians don't actually use their entire "sample" the way statisticians do; even after a first round of selections have been made, there's still far too much information to cope with, so some facts and impressions are selected again to be brought into the foreground of the account.

We do the same thing through common sense. The mind naturally selects some impressions for the foreground, tacitly ignoring the rest. Even someone who possesses vast knowledge — a "broad sample" — doesn't actually use much more knowledge in specific situations than someone who has much less to select from.

But a large supply of knowledge increases the *quality* and *relevance* of those few facts and impressions that can be brought forward and used. Here a better analogy might be a person's wardrobe: people with a lot of clothes don't actually wear more at any given time; the benefit of a large wardrobe is to have just the appropriate piece for any occasion. [78]

Another version of that analogy is that a person with more clothes is better able to incorporate new articles into their wardrobe:

"The more historical knowledge we have, the more we can learn from any given piece of evidence; if we had none, we could learn nothing." So wrote R. G. Collingwood, another

---

78 Borrowed from Emerson's essay on Plato in *Representative Men*.

philosopher of history, who went on to claim that "historical thinking is an original and fundamental idea of the human mind" — something innate or *a priori* — "an idea which every man possesses as part of the furniture of his mind, and discovers himself to possess and in so far as he is conscious of what it is to have a mind."[79]

For both Collingwood and Ortega, it isn't just the past that compels us to study history, but the present and the future. For Collingwood, the study of history begins here and now — or at least we begin by "using the present as evidence for its own past... and any imaginative reconstruction of the past aims at reconstructing the past of this present, the present in which the act of imagination is going on, in which the here-and-now is perceived."

Ortega goes farther, claiming that "life is an activity executed in relation to the future; we find the present or the past afterwards, in relation to that future." More specifically, "it is when I find in the past the means of realizing my future that I discover my present."[80]

Returning to the wardrobe analogy, imagine finding a cool new pair of shoes (or a jacket, or a hat, or suspenders, or whatever) — they seem to be what you've always been looking for. But before making your purchase, you've got to think back to what you already have in the closet that might match. If you don't possess anything that works with those green shoes or pink suspenders, then you lack "the means of realizing your future," and the transaction comes to an end.

Remember that I began this essay with a quote from Lewis Lapham about "defending the future against the past." By claiming the past is something we need to defend against, I take it he's referring to ideas and habits we inherit blindly — the rigid conventions, misleading assumptions, outmoded methods, and ungenerative ideals that promote ignorance, passivity, and helplessness.

---

79 Collingwood quotes are all from the chapter on "Historical Imagination" in *The Idea of History* (1946).

80 Ortega y Gasset, *What is Philosophy* (1964): p. 225.

These ideas probably exist (and persist) because they've been useful. At some time they served a purpose, or helped people find "attainment in the heart of disorder." But ideas, like everything else, have limited lives; eventually they need to be managed, updated, or replaced.

When ideas persist beyond their original purpose, they don't just become useless, they become *worse* than useless: they're an additional burden or constraint, making it even more difficult to make sense of present problems and opportunities.

Arguing this point, Ortega wrote that we grow into a "network of ready-made solutions" before we're even aware of the problems they're supposed to solve. As a result, "when we come to feel actual distress in the face of a vital question, and we really want to find its solution… not only must we struggle with the problem, but we find ourselves caught within the solutions previously received and must also struggle with them."[81]

The best way to avoid this is not with less knowledge, but rather with *more* (or *better* knowledge) by studying history — events we can actually understand — to place ourselves in perspective of a bigger narrative, to think critically about the complex ways in which our biases and assumptions have evolved, and to endow ourselves with richer metaphors and images with which to intermediate past and future ideas.

Apart from getting us out of the "zone of imperfect visibility," thinking through history is a way to cope with our brain's lack of an OFF switch. It's a practice that keeps helps us regulate conceptual consumption, exercise humility and respect life's inevitable anomalies and vicissitudes.

Barzun wrote that history's greatest weakness, "its uncertainty and inability to put things into neat bundles," was also its greatest strength, "its great advantage over ready-made systems." History keeps thinking alive: "Its difficulties force the student's gaze to discern in each event and person its unique character, to mark and remember its own shape. It is a

---

81 Ortega y Gasset, *Man in Crisis* (1962): p. 26.

discipline that strengthens individual judgement and keeps bright the points that connect imagination with present reality."[82]

Emerson, as we might expect, was more poetic in expressing this need: "What is our life but an endless flight of winged facts or events? In splendid variety these changes come, all putting questions to the human spirit. Those men who cannot answer by a superior wisdom these facts or questions of time, serve them. Facts encumber them, tyrannize over them, and make the men of routine, the men of sense, in whom a literal obedience to facts has extinguished every spark of that light by which man is truly man."[83]

That "light by which man is truly man" is the sense of life's incompleteness, by which we define our aspirations. It selects and brings into the foreground those "solitary intimations of a problem… fragments of a yet unknown coherent whole," a compelling mystery which we call the future.

---

82 Barzun, *Of Human Freedom* (1939/1964): p. 181.

83 Emerson, "History" from *Essays: First Series* (1841).

10 Investing in Pragmatic Ideas

Society relies on hard concepts. They're what make language and mathematics so effective. By extension, we rely on them for all of our moral and legal codes, scientific methods, religious doctrines, and literary canons — everything we associate with civilization.

The more rigourous and precise our ideas are, the more effectively we can use and correct them. This is why scientific values and methods have flourished — not just in science but in engineering, business, education, and other fields as well.

But it only goes so far. If the value of rigour and precision is largely in our ability to test and correct, then if we're not open to identifying mistakes and opportunities for improvement, the whole process will start to undermine itself. We might develop very efficient processes for achieving specific ends while lacking any means to assess whether those ends are valid or sustainable.

For example, a professional bodybuilder might use steroids to build muscle more efficiently, while efficiently hastening his own death at the same time. Likewise, financial engineers have become adept at maximizing trading efficiency but it remains to be seen what all the effects of that efficiency will be over the long term of the global economy.

How do we measure and assess not just the effectiveness of our means to specific ends, but their relation to other ends — and the value of pursuing those ends at all? We need better ways to apply a science-like mindset to questions that temporarily defy scientific rigour and quantification. This is where we can use a more pragmatic attitude.

Pragmatism isn't just about "being practical," it's actually a term that originates from philosophy, specifically American philosophy of the late 19th and early 20th century.

William James, who popularized the term, was educated as an M.D. but had no tolerance for the actual practice of medicine. After drifting for much of his late twenties he went on to become a philosopher — hardly a hero to the practical men and women of today.

The old pragmatists like James and Charles S. Peirce were serious scientists and philosophers. They were more concerned with getting things right than getting things done. For Peirce, pragmatism meant making meanings more defined:

"In order to ascertain the meaning of an intellectual conception one should consider what practical consequences might conceivably result by necessity from the truth of that conception; and the sum of these consequences will constitute the entire meaning of the conception."[84]

However, pragmatism is commonly taken to mean the reverse of that — instead of "getting our ideas clear," it's about "getting clear of ideas." One of the definitions of pragmatism I found via Princeton Wordnet is: "guided by practical experience and observation rather than theory."

That intellectually naive attitude can be used very effectively by many personalities who happen to live and work in the right conditions, but those conditions can only be stable for so long, and as things change we need the ability to understand exactly why certain practices worked in the past,

what factors they depend on, and what kind of events might render them less (or more) effective in the future.

This is precisely the challenge we face today. A lot of the conditions that made things work a certain way in the last half of the 20th century have changed. It isn't enough just to make a factory or office run more efficiently every year. It isn't enough just to step on the accelerator (or the brakes) when we confront a challenge. It isn't enough to use the same old, mechanical metaphors.

---

84 "Pragmatism" (1905). *Collected Papers:* v. 5, p. 6.

Read history carefully enough and you'll find that many of the things we take for granted in business, government, and day-to-day life, were once articulated and argued over by philosophers. We don't have to think about them because, centuries ago, someone else already did.

In this way, the so-called practical or action-oriented attitude that renounces reflection doesn't really reject theory, it's rather an unconditional acceptance of theories inherited from the past. To "be practical" means putting absolute, blind faith in someone else's ideas — ideas meant for a different time and place. So ironically, the person who reads and reflects on philosophy is actually more skeptical of philosophy than the person who says it's a waste of time. The untheoretical practitioner trusts ideas blindly, whereas the theoretician tries to get on top of them, to take ownership and manage them more effectively.

Metaphorically, action-oriented people "lease" their theoretical frameworks rather than buying into them directly. This enables them to focus on what they're good at — getting things done — by providing mobility and freedom from the risks and responsibilities of ownership. There's nothing necessarily wrong with being unreflective when it's properly appreciated as just another division of labour in our society. Remember, "do what you do best and link to the rest."

For example, accountants can't afford to worry about a pipe bursting or a roof leaking at tax time; they need to focus on their business and let the property owner take care of the facilities. And most businesses will eventually grow and contract; such periods of change are precisely when a business can least afford to be distracted by peripheral concerns. It's usually preferable to pay an outside specialist who can take care of all the real estate, facilities, groundskeeping, and property matters so you can focus on doing what you're actually paid to do.

Now consider that we also work and live on conceptual grounds, in conceptual facilities that need to be regularly maintained and occasionally renovated or reconstructed.

By "conceptual grounds" and "conceptual facilities" I mean all
the ideas, theories, assumptions, expectations and conventions
that surround us, including all of our assumptions regarding
the aims of enterprise, conventions of success, rules and
unwritten codes of conduct, cultural values and norms,
vocabularies and points of reference, the meanings of words
(such as "goodness" and "truth"), favourite metaphors and
models, objective methods and techniques, subjective
preferences, even the "meaning of life" — anything we can't see
or touch that nonetheless influences our actions and decisions.

Everything we do is saturated in thought and suspended in
language. We can't do anything without some kind of
conceptual framework or background, and we can't do
anything *with* these frameworks and backgrounds without
words and symbols to represent and manage their many
components. These conceptual facilities and grounds are just as
important to working and living as our physical environment
and material tools are; they influence everything we do, and we
can never get completely away from them.

But in comparison to physical facilities, our conceptual facilities
tend to be largely neglected. We can't see and touch them in
quite the same way (or rather, we can't see or touch them at all),
so they're difficult to recognize and grasp — doing so requires
yet another set of conceptual facilities and tools. This is
especially true of those conceptual facilities that touch deeper,
more general levels of life — the stuff that has been maintained
by religions in the past but is increasingly neglected and
shoddily worked over by an ongoing parade of feel-good
books.

Discussing thoughts and knowledge in this way — as if they
exist on a separate level or in a "conceptual sphere" — isn't
necessarily true but it's a practical necessity. Remember the
notion of spatial bias from an earlier chapter: we evolved to
work more effectively with ideas framed in spatial terms. After
all, it isn't the abstract notion of truth that matters most, it's
whether or not the idea tends to survive and reproduce — and
help us do the same.

This in itself demonstrates the point of the chapter. Pragmatism means working with concepts to develop better "for now" solutions to theoretical challenges — equipping them with practical bearings we can observe and use to continue the process through future iterations. Pragmatism isn't just about addressing problems we have now, it's also about being more prepared for those unexpected problems and opportunities we're creating for the future. There's never an expectation of finality. As William James said, by following the pragmatist method,[85]

"Theories thus become instruments, not answers to enigmas, in which we can rest. We don't lie back upon them, we move forward, and, on occasion, make nature over again by their aid. Pragmatism unstiffens all our theories, limbers them up and sets one at work."

This may seem to contradict my earlier claim that new kinds of challenges may need to be addressed by "stiffening" our ideas. But pragmatism doesn't call for a rejection of all rationalizing, it doesn't mean we may not occasionally have to "stiffen" a theory in order to find clarity or generate leverage, it simply calls for a new "attitude of orientation":

"The attitude of looking away from first things, principles, 'categories,' supposed necessities; and of looking towards last things, fruits, consequences, facts ."

Now if looking towards fruits and consequences happens to be most effectively done *using* principles, categories, and supposed necessities *as temporary facilities and tools*, then it is pragmatically acceptable to do so — as long as thinking doesn't get re-oriented back towards "first things" in the process, mistaking an instrument as an ultimate or absolute purpose.

At the same time, pragmatism shouldn't be mistaken as an excuse to walk away from theory and logic altogether; that would assume that pragmatism is *a priori* the best way of thinking, that our best practices are already worked out and settled — which is exactly the kind of assumption that

---

85 This quote and the one following are from *Pragmatism: A New Name for Some Old Ways of Thinking* (1907).

pragmatism is meant to root out and overcome. To take pragmatism as absolutely *the* best practice would present it as an absurd contradiction. An absolute principle that advocates rejecting all absolute principles must itself be rejected, according to itself.

Whereas if we learn to appreciate pragmatism as an attitude or disposition, and we outgrow the reliance on principles and rules to grant us *permission* to get on with things — in other words, if we learn to appreciate the process as an end in itself, not requiring rational validation — then the contradiction becomes relatively unimportant, personally.

The pragmatist appreciation of truth-in-the-making is a realization by the pragmatist individual that they have grown beyond absolute reliance on principles; their mind has developed enough to move about on its own legs; principles have become internalized as a part of that movement instead of being external supports.

Pragmatism means taking ownership of one's own conceptual facilities and grounds, accounting for them objectively, putting them "on the books" as assets.

This in turn incurs a lifelong obligation or debt that pragmatists must pay. To get away with saying that truth is in the making, *you've got to actually keep making it*, you've got to keep working with it and maintaining it, continuing to cover the costs, paying down the mortgage, and reinvesting. Owning your own knowledge is an ongoing commitment, not an instantaneous achievement.

If you claim to be a pragmatist but don't accept this attitude of ongoing ownership and responsibility by continually updating, maintaining, and buying into your conceptual facilities — if you become too carefree about the pragmatist contradiction (i.e. if you say, "Truth is in the making, the only absolute truth is that there is no absolute truth, so let's not bother") — then you end up with nothing sustainable.

There's nothing inherently wrong with that. You can walk away from all this intellectual stuff and be purely action-oriented if you like, but you can't claim it's because you took possession of some ultimate knowledge, principle, or rationale. If you walk away from the truth and truthmaking altogether, you can only claim specific practical or arbitrary reasons, not superior knowledge or understanding.

You could claim you simply *feel* like letting it go, or you could say it's because you're already in the habit of letting others take care of theoretical concerns, or you could say it's because you're just going along with everybody around you, or you could claim that your decision is based on some immediate necessity or benefit (i.e. "I don't have time for that; there are other things I should be doing"), but any general rationalization of the decision not to care about theory and truth would be absurd.

I've heard self-identified "practical" people make general statements about the superiority of "practice vs. theory," but it's absurd to give *theoretical reasons* for not being concerned with theoretical reasoning.

Theory is itself a kind of practice, in the most general sense of the word. Theory and practice aren't opposed. Being concerned with theoretical knowledge, truthmaking and thought does not necessarily mean being impractical. Theory is a different, more general kind of practice aimed at designing and maintaining the conceptual facilities through which we work, learn, and live.

As I use the term, theory is the practice of using language to make our ideas manageable and clear. It's about seeing. A theory works like a lens to help us focus only on features that will make us most effective. Like any other practice, it can be done with varying degrees of competence. Mastery requires sustained practice through a variety of challenges. It's like trying to draw a two-dimensional picture of a three-dimensional scene. There are techniques and principles of perspective that need to be learned to depict the world realistically, and to indicate where different objects are in relation to each other.

There's nothing inherently wrong with neglecting theory for the sake of focusing on real action; but there *is* something wrong with presuming to have a firm grasp of both aspects, claiming to own knowledge that you never had to pay for and don't actively maintain.

It becomes a kind of intellectual vagrancy. It's dangerous because it puts blind trust in mysterious and unaccountable sources of ideas. When things start to change or go awry, intellectually vagrant individuals (or organizations) get pushed around by events and have almost no recourse but to hope the system becomes somewhat stable soon so they can find another bit of shelter to occupy.

By "intellectually vagrant," I have in mind stereotypical business people driven by short-term results or dreams of fast financial freedom. The business realm isn't the only place we find these people (politics comes to mind as well), but they're easiest to tell this story about.

What sets them apart from more honest executives and practitioners (or "tenants," who lease their conceptual facilities because they openly admit it isn't their business to manage them), is that vagrants actually claim to *know* their actions are grounded in truth.

Here I'm thinking especially of certain gross simplifications of pseudo-Darwinian ethics — i.e. "everything is governed by the profit motive," "greed is good," "eat or be eaten," etc. Enron's CEO Jeffrey Skilling famously admired Richard Dawkins's *Selfish Gene*, falsely interpreting the theory to mean that societies ought to be organized around selfish motives. Ultimately Enron became a lesson about what "survival of the fittest" really means: not necessarily survival of the strongest, smartest, and most aggressive, but survival of the most suited to circumstances — which often means kindest, most cooperative, and luckiest.[86]

Paradoxically, what intellectual vagrants claim to know tends to become a supposed excuse to not have to learn any more. They don't ask hard questions, they don't sympathize with other viewpoints. They just tell themselves they're right and

---

86 See "Darwin Misunderstood" by Michael Shermer for *Scientific American* (February 2009). For an account of this error's role in Enron's downfall see *Enron: The Smartet Guys in the Room* (2003, 2005 film).

blaze on, creating dangerous social and ethical structures that put others at risk as well.

The big problem with such false claims to owning knowledge is that honest practitioner-tenants get fooled into working and living in the same derelict conceptual facilities. When the pipes burst and the roof starts leaking, nobody's going to fix it. At best, problems might get a temporary patch or cover-up, which may keep the facilities operational and seemingly in good order; but they might get repaired in a way that makes them less functional in the long run, so one day the whole thing could just collapse and leave nothing behind where the tenants once thought they were safe.

Of course, to say these collapses leave nothing behind at all is an exaggeration. They often leave behind pieces of infrastructure, resources, and knowledge to benefit former competitors, successors and other emerging enterprises. At the very least, such collapses educate survivors and observers, who may learn something from the mistakes, and might even find a few good pieces of ideas in the debris.

But it's important to recognize that knowledge — like any other kind of resource or infrastructure — is most beneficial when it's functionally integrated into a larger system. Specifically, events are most educative when they confirm, refute, or refine knowledge we already have.

Without existing knowledge, events will occur to us merely as a few disconnected anecdotes and facts — which will probably soon be forgotten without any context to relate them to. Someone who had never thought much about business (or ethics, or culture, or psychology) is unlikely to learn much from the Enron fiasco, or the tech bubble, or the housing bubble, or the credit crunch, or the investment banking collapse, or whatever comes next. Whereas someone who already knows a lot about an event's context might learn enough from it to fill a whole book — or even a whole academic career.

To fully understand events, it's especially important to articulate assumptions, expectations, or speculations about how things might turn out in the future — *before* they turn out — and why you think that way. By doing so, the future becomes a kind of objective scorekeeper that provides indications of how well our ideas are performing, helping us overcome the subjective weaknesses in our knowledge, notifying us to ideas and assumptions that need to be improved, refined, expanded, updated, opened up, or shut down.

Think of how much life goes by without being harnessed for educational or intellectual use. There are ways to turn anything towards more generative, sustainable, and manageable ends. All experience is in a sense *learning experience*, but it is predominantly undisciplined and unproductive; we tend to let most things come and go without affecting our theories.

Meanwhile, we allow ideas and habits to become important parts of our lives without *accounting* for them. We learn some of our most influential habits, preferences, and beliefs by accident. Most people have no clue how these were formed, nor would they know how to evaluate or correct them.

When these habits, preferences, and beliefs are challenged, people will stand up for "who they are," they'll go to war over "what they believe," but they are hardly able to make any account of the sources of their identity or beliefs, nor make the even the minutest adjustments needed to turn a destructive confrontation into a generative conversation. Instead, most people are content merely to be "who they are," and "agree to disagree" with anyone who's different. This goes nowhere.

The ultimate good of pragmatism isn't profit or truth; the ultimate good of pragmatism is found in social aspects — i.e. conversation and collaboration — which are ultimately what life is all about.

Pragmatism is the attitude by which we humanize the organizations and institutions where we work, learn, and live. As these institutions become more humane, it becomes easier to be humane ourselves. As we "unstiffen our theories" we become more able to communicate and collaborate — resolving differences, overcoming challenges, and addressing new opportunities, both in our private lives and as part of larger public enterprise.

A pragmatic plasticity is required to be both tough and soft — rigid at times and malleable at others. On one hand we need to use hard facts and rules to avoid or overcome subjective excesses. On the other hand, the desired aim of life *is* subjective well-being and freedom.

So I'm going to suggest a couple of terms to describe two complementary aspects of my pragmatic approach: "open objectivity" and "temperate subjectivity." Temperate subjectivity is the desired end, and open objectivity is the means to that end. Or relating them to the terms of a previous chapter, we ought to conceive a good life as a regulated and steady current flowing through clearly defined yet open and adaptable frameworks.

Open objectivity recognizes that we can't accomplish anything together unless we have hard structures and facts to serve as common points of reference. When disputes arise, we need to be able to say, "Well, let's see how X turns out, then we'll know if either one of us is right." But this is no way to enjoy life; merely knowing what's right and following hard rules is not the whole point of living, so this objectivity needs to be open-ended, incomplete, liberating.

The aim is to condition ourselves to make intuitive, spontaneous decisions and evaluations that are just as valid and effective as those calculated by the objective instruments we design. This is what I mean by temperate subjectivity, whereby free thinking has been informed by objective structures and facts, and those structures and facts are always readily available to check ourselves against the possibility of repeating past mistakes.

Creative freedom is experienced as enjoyable in itself, and it also serves practical necessities — just like owning your own home. At its simplest, a good and happy life is about having the freedom (which, don't forget, also means having security and stability) to enjoy spontaneous moments of beauty, discovery, laughter, and love.

At the same time, emergencies and surprises inevitably occur, whether we want them to or not, and these can't be totally accounted for, objectively, in advance. The most effective decisions are often made by people who have been conditioned through objective frameworks to intuitively know what to do without being paralysed by analysis and deliberation.

Ultimately, a society of human minds is smarter than anything we could ever design. But our minds can't function without conceptual facilities — ideas, concepts, theories — and these facilities *are* designed. If they're designed poorly, we think poorly; if they're designed well, we think well. Pragmatism reframes the world so instead of "problems" we see opportunities to learn.

When thinking is done well, we can use it to turn even more of life into a fulfilling, generative experience.

11 The Medium of Social Currency

In the late 90s there was considerable hype about a new economy with new rules until the tech bubble collapsed in 2000/2001. A lot of people from the old-school thought that disaster would discredit the entire movement, but it didn't — at least not any more than the housing/finance collapse discredited the notion of home ownership.

Through the bust we were able to learn what was actually viable online. A few companies like Google, eBay and Amazon kept growing; a new generation of startups was emerging, bringing back a sense of enthusiasm, focusing on a new paradigm.

The biggest mistake concerning the web has been to conceive it as merely a more efficient way to do things that were already done offline. We limit ourselves by thinking of websites as paperless catalogues, paperless newspapers and paperless books; computers are not just paperless typewriters, paperless filing cabinets and paperless mailboxes. The most effective ways to use computers and cell phones are in an ongoing process of being discovered. It's an ongoing experiment; it's an adventure.

Consider Facebook, which was conceived (or at least named) after old-fashioned student directories, but quickly went far beyond that static model. The value of Facebook isn't that it stores contacts and photos; its genuine value is in the streams of fresh experience it provides for users.

It requires a conceptual leap from a static mindset towards a more dynamic one. You can't just begin with inert models and then add motion to them, you need to overcome those blockish notions altogether and get immersed in the living, breathing, undulating system.

However, much of the "news" in a newspaper needs to be updated and revised before it even reaches your door — for example, Olympic medal standings. Printed news doesn't fl ow very well with actual events.

The new ways of delivering news online are able to fl ow and stay current with ongoing events while dynamically addressing the customized needs of different people. Rather than simply posing a threat to newspapers and TV, blogs and other new media online might actually save professional journalism by making it more effective and relevant to our lives than ever.

We're not there yet, and effective progress isn't guaranteed; new technology might defeat its own purpose if we don't take responsibility for making it function effectively. We need to be open to the unexpected value created by new media while building on the value that has already been established by the old media.

But it's hard. Modifying Homer Simpson's famous quip about alcohol, technology is "the cause of — and solution to — all of life's problems."

The same force that's generating the fl ood of information is also producing tools to direct it into more manageable channels. And then we find ourselves on a treadmill, still facing the same problem, still making an effort to address it but not getting any closer to solving it. These applications and services don't *necessarily* reduce the volume of information; they also increase it.

Perhaps the best demonstrations of this paradox are services like FriendFeed and Google Buzz, which aggregate all of a person's online content (pictures, videos, events, blog posts, bookmarks, tweets, shared items, comments, etc.) from the various social applications into one feed, which in turn is aggregated with the feeds of other people to be followed by friends, fans, voyeurs, etc.

Even some of the most prolific users of social media originally complained that FriendFeed is very noisy and just adds to the burden of being online. As with anything, it all depends on what you do with it. Services like FriendFeed, Buzz, and

Google Wave represent an issue that encompasses the entire Web: we're just beginning to appreciate its capabilities and master the new kinds of skills needed to use it effectively.

The people who thrive in Web-related enterprises are successful largely because they know they don't know how their projects will turn out. Great hackers and entrepreneurs know they'll be learning on the fly. They expect to encounter unexpected setbacks that will require nimble adaptations. And sometimes they persist *because* of those challenges, not just despite them.

This lesson about innovation and education is the soil in which all subsequent lessons about making something on the Web must be sown. Without it there can be very little growth. Without it, to paraphrase a remark from Marshall McLuhan, we see things "through the spectacles of the preceding age," like military strategists who are "magnifi cently prepared to fight the previous war."[87] By the time these designs and plans are executed they're already becoming obsolete.

Consider how Associated Press interpreted fi ndings in "A New Model for News: Studying the Deep Structure of Young-Adult News Consumption," a report they released in June 2008.[88]

The report includes some interesting points and valuable insights, but it seems to harbour some deeply embedded, tacit assumptions about news that keep its thinking lodged in the past. Its findings seem to validate my belief that the whole conceptual map for dealing with news needs to be redrawn. While they pick up on some landmark features of the present, they fail to orient them in a way that leads to the future.

Among the present findings is that "news is connected to e-mail." This could simply be a technical matter: news and email happen to "come in small snippets of information" and share the same medium of delivery, the report explains. Many of the subjects in the ethnographic research found themselves looking at headlines that happened to be handy when checking Yahoo Mail or their PDA.

---

87 Marshall McLuhan, *Understanding Media* (1964/1994, MIT): p. 243.
88 Published June 2008 at http://www.ap.org/newmodel.pdf

But what the report fails to address is that email is essentially a kind of news; it's tricky to draw a clear distinction between them — which isn't to say we should not make a distinction; it's only to point out that the AP report doesn't, and therefore misses valuable insight.

It could be argued that the degree to which news differs from email is proportionate with the degree to which news fails to capture people's attention and interest. If you want to know why people don't care about "the News," write down your definition of what makes it different from personal messages and conversations. You've just written down a list of reasons why people don't care about news.

The notion that news exists on a plane apart from people's actual lives is the core assumption of the old media that needs to be discarded. Here we find the "spectacles of the preceding age" worn by folks reared in old media organizations.

One could be forgiven for not noticing that the conventional distinction between the News and our actual lives is itself largely a result of technology (language, the printing press, broadcasting) that developed just as helplessly as it is now being broken down. The News of old was as much of an ongoing experiment as the Web — or rather, the web is simply the latest iteration.

Society in general has been an ongoing experiment, and the evolving means of communication have always set the basic pattern for every age.

An article Jack Shafer wrote for Slate argued that the value of newspapers has been the "social currency" they provide for our actual lives. News items were like tokens to exchange with people encountered in the course of daily business.

At the peak of newspapers' influence, everyone could assume that almost everyone else would be familiar with some of the content from that day's paper – "that picture of an egg frying on a city street the paper published; or a comment about a movie review or comic strip; or an opinion about local government based on a piece by a political columnist" [89] — and new relationships developed according to what was said about these common points of reference.

Now the way information is proliferating and diverging into various channels, we don't all share the same social currency, and it's increasingly difficult to find shared points of reference. Without common references, it's difficult to generate conversation with new contacts and get a sense of who they are, and then it's nearly impossible to establish trust and build relationships – not to mention communities.

This function is increasingly being distributed through online social networking platforms like Facebook and Twitter. The information in people's pages and profiles (including the lists of people who are already friends) is the new social currency... or is it?

Writing at his own site, Economic Principals, David Warsh built on Shafer's piece to ague that "Newspapers Are [Still] the Central Banks of Social Currency." [90] It's a good argument; it made me take a step back and re-think my ideas.

Adding my own interpretation to Warsh's metaphor, I wrote that much of the social networking sphere is a fast-paced-yet-going-nowhere derivatives market. Automated tools for aggregating, recommending and rating mostly keep the sub-prime content moving fast enough to save anyone from truly being aware of the the burdens and risks of ownership — the cost of actually having to think — or so we let ourselves assume.

As we have witnessed over the past couple of years in financial markets, this high-volume/high-efficiency set of practices is not sustainable. We need to build social capital that holds real value despite ups-and-downs in the cultural marketplace of ideas and opinions.

---

89 "What's Really Killing Newspapers?" by Jack Shafer on slate.com (Aug. 1, 2008).

90 "Newspapers are the Central Banks of Social Currency," by David Warsh at economicprincipals.com (Aug. 18, 2008).

Obviously we can't turn back time and undo the technological advances that put us in the position of having to cope with so much information. The best strategies for dealing with it will emerge from the advancements themselves (while building on the social capital they inherit from the past, and staying open to advancements that will continue to evolve).

Remember in an earlier chapter I argued that the most important development isn't merely the technology itself but how it affects our mental models: the notion of streams and threads of information — as in blogs, discussion forums, and mini-feeds on Facebook — is a very useful metaphor to help us make sense of personal identity and social relationships in our complex modern world, both on- and off-line.

Begin with the concept of a "lifestream."[91] The best example of a lifestream is probably a personal feed on FriendFeed. Increasingly, Facebook is a kind of lifestream too.

A lifestream is a continuous record of the events of one's life, as they're represented and aggregated from various social media services people might belong to. These events don't have to be all that meaningful or important, and most of them are excruciatingly mundane — a fact that critics begrudge and use to argue that lifestreams are stupid — but it seems obvious to me that the first step towards making one's life more meaningful is to get a sense of all the associated information in an orderly way, which is something that lifestreaming can help do.

When all we can see is what's happening *at a given moment*, we tend to follow the crowd: we fail to develop the ability to think, work, learn, and live apart from that crowd. But when we can view our own actions *playing out over time* in one continuous thread, as in a lifestream, we get a better idea of who we are (or perhaps *aren't*). Then we can stop following the crowd from fad to fad and ground ourselves via sustainable personal identities,

---

91 The term was coined by Eric Freeman and David Gelerntner, based on ideas explored in Gelerntner's *Mirror Worlds* (1992), and formalized in "The Lifestreams Software Architecture," Freeman's doctoral dissertation at Yale University (1997).

each with our own respective knowledge, skills, styles and voices that nobody else can duplicate exactly.

The thread metaphor is especially valuable when we try to make sense of the relation between personal and social aspects of living, or the relation between "the individual" and "the group."

The value of self-reliance is not merely personal or individualistic. When we each cultivate distinctive talents and personal mastery for ourselves, our society becomes richer and more resilient. The greater degree of variety of knowledge and competence is present in a group, the more likely the group is to survive and thrive via changing opportunities and challenges.

Hence a *social fabric* develops as our many personal threads distribute evenly across the full range of experience — not tangling too close together or leaving too many gaps, but each tending to find an individual niche within reach of others but with room to move and grow. It's just as important that our threads should all continually stretch towards the future, learning and growing via new challenges, rather than going in circles, or falling slack and getting tied into knots.

My notion of the role of news is that it provides the perpendicular threads that weave our lives into a coherent fabric. Without these common cross-references it's diffi cult to maintain an even distribution. Without objective threads being weaved laterally, the fabric may disintegrate into separate bunches, tangles, and braids.

News about the world and streams of personal experience aren't separate things. I think the best way to describe them is to use William James's analogy, describing "the conterminousness of different minds" as like a geometric point that is not self-sufficient but is defined by lines intersecting *through* it.[92] The *point* of any given event isn't merely abstract news, nor is it merely a matter of personal interest; it's where the two aspects merge.

---

92 William James, "A World of Pure Experience" (1904), from *William James: The Essential Writings*, Bruce Wilshire, ed. (1984): p. 196.

Media in its essence is simply the means by which we place ourselves in the world by placing events, people, and ideas in relation to each other.

As we communicate through the course of the day, we each have a personal responsibility to continually weave information into this general fabric — interpreting each moment into knowledge that can be extended both spatially and temporally, generating relevance and meaning in the process, leaving some aspect of the thread open to the future.

We can't choose whether or not to participate. We're already thrown into it and presented the choice of whether to participate more or less generatively, more or less effectively through the connections we make and the stories those connections represent. There are a couple of very basic factors determining we *must* always compose narratives.

The first factor is time — not just something we live in, but a quality that affects our minds, our nervous systems, and all of our experience. We have no choice but to think and feel because thinking and feeling naturally happen and there's no way to turn them off. We can learn to think and feel certain ways with some regularity, we can direct our attention and we can think of ways to dismiss facts as "nothings," but we can't think nothing in the literal sense of not thinking at all.

The second factor is evolution — itself made necessary by the universal qualities of time. Our ancestors' propensity to turn facts and experience into ideas and stories enabled our species to flourish and now we're stuck with that nature. We can't help wanting to know and tell it because individuals with the know-and-tell genes probably had more grandchildren (and great-grandchildren, and friends, etc) and were more effective cooperators when it came time to help each other build and protect each other in battle.

In other words, that feeling of "I have to tweet about this!" has the same source as the impulse our ancestors had to share heroic tales and local lore from generation to generation — stories that became focal points for shared social identity and perhaps the biggest reason our species (and certainly our civilization) is here to talk, tweet, and write about it today.

Think back to the earlier chapter on the "will to relevance." The urge to document and share knowledge is largely innate. We don't even need to resort to a scientific explanation. Just take a look at what happens in coffee shops and how people spontaneously use the web to socialize. The evidence is all around us.

Like history, journalism involves much more than merely maintaining a record of facts — if only because people often disagree on what happened and how to emphasize particular aspects over others. More important is that we don't tend to stop at just "keeping a record": we're also inclined to interpret. We form predictions, opinions, and arguments in the process. Facts take on different meanings depending on how they're focused on and framed.

Life comes out looking different when we try to capture and represent it. Every kind of media has specific properties that affect how things appear through it. Just as painters use linear perspective to convey depth, colour theory to convey light, and other tricks to suggest form and action, there's a lot of artifice in stories and theories that appear true-to-life.

Good journalists, historians, philosophers, and poets don't always work with straight lines; they bend things a little, so when we look at them they'll appear simple.

So when we have opportunities to shape our narratives and theories we need to consider what effects they'll have on our future thoughts and feelings.

It's as if you're constantly crafting the lens through which you'll observe the next moment, the next crisis, the next opportunity, the next period of your life — as well as how you'll remember the current one. You're also shaping the lens through which others will observe and remember *you*.

These duties aren't reserved for professionals. In a digital world we're all becoming novelists, composing the stories of our lives — not just metaphorically, but literally. Our online stories are documented and persistent; they also have immediate and often significant effects — think of internet memes and market fluctuations — on the character of our society.

Every click is a vote, every link is a nomination of something you want others to invest their attention in, incorporate into their stories, and carry into the future. Our decisions have always had these kinds of effects; the web just makes the process more explicit and profound. These new realities give us both the opportunity and the need to be more responsible for how our stories turn out.

Maybe we should think of ourselves as critics, rather than only "novelists-of-ourselves." Novels exist independently, between two covers, whereas our lives are entailed in a complex, dynamic web of relationships. Simply defining our place within the web is a challenge in itself. This is what criticism essentially means. As Richard Rorty, one of the heroes of this book suggested, criticism isn't about explaining or evaluating; criticism foremost means "placing books in the context of other books, figures in the context of other figures."[93]

In a sense, science is just this kind of criticism as performed on life's temporal aspect: placing events in the context of other events, factors in the context of other factors, conditions in the context of other conditions, effects in the context of causes. History and journalism serve the same function: distinguishing the critical moments. It's all storytelling — which isn't to say that anything goes. The more precisely our knowledge accords with observable realities, the more open our ideas are to falsification and refinement by others (again, with reference to observable realities), the more generative and sustainable the process and our relationships will be.

We need to focus on fostering that open objectivity; subjective benefits will follow. We don't need to worry as much about whether momentum or motivation will persist. Force and drive are over-rated. The world is not going to stop. Things have always happened and things will continue happening as long as time exists.

What we do need to worry about is how we frame things — ensuring our ideas and practices aren't just efficient and precise but compatible, consistent, and coherent as well. That's our

---

93 Richard Rorty, *Contingency, Irony, and Solidarity* (1989): p. 80.

responsibility: outlining the relations and distinctions among things, people, ideas, and events, in order to find the gaps that need to be filled. Frame those problems and opportunities right and the rest should start to follow naturally.

This is all media is to me: simply the means by which we place ourselves in relation to others — on a personal level, discovering and defining ourselves through the process of selecting and signalling our affinities and associations — and on the social level, ultimately placing the present in relation to the past and the future.[94]

---

94 At this point I should recognize some similarities with the work of Anthony Giddens, specifically my discussion of narrative self-identity is reminiscent of parts of his *Modernity and Self-Identity* (1991), e.g. on p. 215. However, I haven't had an opportunity to explore these similarities in depth (just as members of Giddens's generation have perhaps neglected Ortega and other older thinkers whom I've found value in).

12 Truth, Will & Relevance

My aim here has not been to establish a coherent system, but rather to lay out a generative background for overcoming mistaken biases and assumptions. The value in the notion of will to relevance is not that it accurately explains or proves a lot of specific things; its value is that it leads me to think more carefully. It keeps me grounded — in the sense that we ground electrical currents.

This is not a foundation, it's a way to keep ideas flowing — remember that what's difficult one moment might be a gratifying challenge after a few other things are tried, learned, or overcome — while channelling the most dubious or dangerous ideas out of the way.

It's as much about epistemology as it is about psychology. It's about truth — or at least working towards truth, or being ready for when truth might unexpectedly appear. It prevents me from either trusting old assumptions or getting too excited by new ideas.

It comes down to a concern that I might mistakenly believe ideas to be right and true when in fact they only satisfy a need to feel more relevant. I caught myself doing this when I was much younger, calling it "the architect's ego" after noticing my inclination to design idealistic social structures was a direct extension of my passion for architecture and physical design. In some aspects both enterprises come from the same source. Aesthetics can have a powerful affect on ideas and beliefs.

So I asked myself, "What if all of my ideas merely fulfill my personal need to produce aesthetically pleasing things?" When I took a serious look at my ideas through that lens, I started to find I was in love with ideas that were not particularly valid or useful. I loved them merely because they were *my* ideas, and I had been seduced and flattered into overlooking a lot of their flaws.

And I'm not the only one. Every day I see people promoting an idea not because it's more valid but because it's theirs and it fulfills their need to feel effective and relevant.

We often see groups from younger generations avidly promoting new ideas and practices, and I suspect this has as much to do with their frustration at feeling irrelevant in the old system, less to do with the actual merits of the ideas and practices. This is not a new suggestion, but I think it's more useful to ground it in the theory of relevance to make it continuous with the rest of human behaviour.

Conversely, established groups in older generations who oppose reform aren't necessarily basing their ideas on merit either. As often as not they seem to be trying to maintain their old networks of relevance (both social and conceptual networks) rather than bothering to make an honest evaluation and accommodation to emerging opportunities and challenges.

In the past we've talked about this behaviour in terms of desire to "hold power" (or in the case of reformers, to "gain power"). I try to avoid those terms.

By framing it as relevance and effectiveness instead of power we have a more effective way to evaluate and reconcile the desires of different groups. Instead of talking about "who *is* right" or "who *has* the right" to power, we should ask, what effects will occur if we change or don't change, and how do our decisions affect future frames and flows of relevance.

This way of thinking is as much a practice as it is a theory. Over time I've learned to turn this thinking back on itself, as a way to catch the biases and infatuations that might affect my own ideas, as if they themselves are parasitically lodged in the mind, trying to make themselves more relevant at the expense of generative progress.

This is really the key point: whatever it is that motivates us, is motivating me as I write this, and it's motivating you as you're reading and thinking about it too. We need keep ourselves actively aware of the heuristics and biases that creep into our stories and ideas.

Maybe even all of the ideas in this book are misleading. I don't assume they're perfect. But these ideas — the last notion especially — unlike other ideas, compel me to *keep looking and asking*, which is often the best we can do in the face of such profound uncertainty.

It comes down to education as a way of life: keeping the love of learning alive, fostering both the spirit of adventure *and* the will for discipline. This is the vision I find in my favourite thinkers, both ancient and modern.

As I read John Dewey's *Democracy and Education*, for example, I got a sense that for Dewey, education is itself a kind of religion. As I read further I found he was even more explicit about it. In an essay titled "What I Believe," he directly challenged the basic assumption that life must be lived for the sake of something supernatural, or outside of experience, arguing we can cultivate worthwhile meanings and values through experience itself by applying open, scientific, pragmatic methods, as "means to a fuller and more significant future experience." This process of discovery isn't merely useful, it's a sufficient source of joy in itself. [95]

Peirce suggested it could be said that "there is but one thing needful for learning the truth, and that is a hearty and active desire to learn what is true." Inquiry at its fullest "has the vital power of self-correction and of growth," because "no matter how erroneous your ideas of the method may be at first, you will be forced at length to correct them so long as your activity is moved by that sincere desire." [96]

We can debate until we're dead about whether truth is known by induction, deduction, abduction, falsification, or first principles. Ultimately no theory or method alone (or in any *fixed* combination) will provide a formula for determining the truth.

Our ideas and methods are all conceptual tools — no more and no less — varying in applicability, depending on the factors

---

95 "What I Believe" (1930) in *The Essential Dewey,* Hickman & Alexander ed. (1998): V. 1, p. 25.

96 "The First Rule of Logic" (1898) in *Collected Papers*: V. 8, p. 405.

present in particular situations and subordinate to our intrinsic desire to make our ideas mutually relevant and outwardly effective.

There is no cause for despair here. The faith we place in ideas is not exactly misplaced, it's merely *misidentified*. While we might feel like it's our ideas we trust, it's actually *ourselves* we trust.

If you genuinely believe you have a great idea, look at that as a reflection of your ability rather than the idea itself — and not an ability that you can take for granted, but an ability that requires development and ongoing discipline. We've produced a lot of great ideas, we have no reason to doubt our ability to produce better ones in the future — as long as we don't get arrogant, and as long as we don't let our ideas use us more effectively than we use them.

13 The Purpose of Life

When I tried to understand "what it's all about" a few years ago I came to the conclusion that the purpose of life is to tell a good story.

This is far from an original idea — there is no shortage of literature dealing with the notion that life is essentially narrative — but a true appreciation of it is something we each have to arrive at through our own experience.

Some people are drawn to the amusing and irreverent; some are drawn to stories about risk and accomplishment — competitive victories and feats of ingenuity or perseverance — and some are drawn to stories about love, relationships, and unity.

Whatever you're drawn to, regardless of what you believe, all the other purposes in life — happiness, utility, love, success, discovery, survival, procreation… are just special kinds of stories.

Even more broadly, stories *must* occur. Unlike other presumed aims, such as happiness or utility, it isn't about having stories or no stories, it's about continuing, expanding, and refining the stories that are already given to us. [97]

At the very least, you can't deny that we have an instinct for stories, deeply embedded by our nature. [98] So story is the purpose *of* life while happiness etc are purposes *in* life. Other purposes are present but not all-encompassing.

Of course, we're still free to enjoy and make use of all the diverse purposes *in* life, so you can still go ahead and aim for a great career and a family with the woman or man of your

---

97 Charles Taylor excellently describes the necessity of the narrative aspect of human experience in *Sources of the Self* (1989): p. 46 - 52. I'm also aware that Jean-Francois Lyotard and other postmodern theorists have already covered this ground in their own style.

98 Bryan Boyd, *On the Origin of Stories* (2009).

dreams (or you can cure cancer or serve God or visit every country in the world or even stay at home eating cheeseburgers every day, if that's the best story you can come up with) but the story-purpose grounds them all, puts them all in the same general frame.

Beyond that, some stories are better than others. Our aim should be for *good* stories — or *better* stories... But who's to decide what's a good story?

It's largely subjective. Much of it comes down to working out for ourselves what's good and what's bad, *learning* what's good and bad is itself part of the story.

There is an objective aspect as well. Some stories are more effective and generative[99] than others — which is to say, some stories acquire a life of their own, proliferating and generating useful outcomes and positive effects — and in this way we're saved from the despair of "agreeing to disagree."

The outcome that matters most is the ability to make our stories even better. When trying to decide how to approach things, we should ask, "Does this experience... not just make for a good story in itself — but does it help me choose and affect the kinds of other stories I want to tell in the future? Does it help define my character and generate meaning?"

And it isn't just about one's self. This is one of the most important lessons we're learning by using the Web: it's about how relevant we become among others, which is measured by how much others can take away from us — "take away" in a nonrivalrous sense: something complementary, like knowledge, that many people can possess in common.

---

99 My use of "generative" refers to two different meanings at once: 1) by way of Dan McAdams [see *The Redemptive Self* (2006); originally used by Erik Erikson in *Childhood and Society* (1963)] referring to a concern for the well-being of future generations; 2) from Jonathan Zittrain, referring to "generative technologies" like the PC and the Internet that "produce unanticipated change through unfiltered contributions from broad and varied audiences" [*The Future of the Internet--And How to Stop It* (2008): p. 70]. I will continue to integrate these notions in my ongoing research, practice, conversations, and writing.

Tell a story that someone else can incorporate into their own life, work, and education. Tell a story that relates to the story of our time — whatever that might turn out to be. Participate in something bigger than one's self. Tell a story that outlives us and becomes something that later generations can build on — not in a way we can possibly anticipate or determine, but in a way they can discover and create for themselves as they see how history unfolds and notice the things that we're missing.

We always need to leave a little bit open. We always need to leave at least a little room for surprise, adventure, and opportunities to learn. If we don't allow room for uncertainty, ambiguity, and unexpected change in our social structures, something will eventually come along and change things from the outside, with more devastating effects.

Uncertainty isn't something to avoid at all costs. Uncertainty, or at least dramatic tension, is an inherent quality of life — and an essential element of any good story.

After all, would life be worth living if we already knew how it's all going to turn out?

• • •

Big thanks to my family & friends for your patience, and to everyone who commented and criticized along the way.

There's still a lot to say and do...

more » **brianfrank.ca**/truth-will-relevance